THE JAMIE KENNEDY
COOKBOOK

Toronto
Oxford University Press
1985

For Cynthia and Julia

Thanks to Richard Teleky and Sally Livingston of Oxford University Press, and to all the chefs, colleagues, family and friends who have helped me throughout my career, making this book possible.

Art work for the opening pages of each chapter has been adapted from Palmerston's logo, designed by Bruna Franceschini.

Cover photograph by Robert Wigington.

CANADIAN CATALOGUING IN PUBLICATION DATA
Kennedy, Jamie.
The Jamie Kennedy cookbook
Includes index.
ISBN 0-19-540471-8
1. Cookery.   I. Title.
TX715.K46 1985   641.5   C85-099417-9

OXFORD is a trademark of Oxford University Press
1 2 3 4 — 8 7 6 5
Printed in Canada by Webcom Ltd

CONTENTS

INTRODUCTION

My career in cooking started in the dormitory of a private, co-ed prep school in Connecticut, where I was boarding. They fed us cafeteria food, the kind of stuff Holden Caulfield ate in *The Catcher in the Rye*. One night a few of us set our alarms for 1:00 a.m. so we could get up and cook. This was the time of fondue bourguignon sets—somebody had one and we sneaked good-quality beef, peanut oil, and cases of beer into the dorm. All of us put in a few bucks for this clandestine party, and I looked up recipes for the bourguignon sauces and made them in my room. That's when it struck me how people respond to something good to eat, how you can please people with food. I ended up founding the school's Culinary Club. When I graduated, and my parents moved back to Toronto, I went with them instead of going directly to university—something almost unheard of in my class. I planned to work for a year, then maybe go to Europe. One of the first people I spoke to about a job was Herbert Sonzogni, chef at the Windsor Arms Hotel, now chef-patron of Babsi's in Mississauga. He said "You like cooking?" with a big laugh, and warned me how tough it was. Then he asked that I sign an apprenticeship contract for three years—he probably expected me to last a couple of weeks. I started working nights in the Three Small Rooms as an apprentice to the saucier. I liked that work but always watched the sous chef, Ulrich Herzig (now Executive Chef at the Prince Hotel), who became the most influential person in my training. He noticed me looking—he was making terrines, galantines, doing it in the most fastidious, immaculate style you could imagine. It was like a dance—perfect. He was temperamental and demanded that everyone around him keep the same standards, even if it took an unreasonable amount of time. One day he asked if I'd like to work with him. He taught me the rudiments of cooking—not what you do at the stove, but how to organize: how to arrange for the boning of three cases of chicken so that every part is used for something, how to monitor what we had in the refrigerator, how to work in a production mode. Cooking in a sensible fashion. He also emphasized the basics of working with food, knowing how it reacts. Eventually this freed me to be innovative and use these skills to express myself. Of course the whole process took an apprenticeship and years of working with other fine chefs.

After four years at the Windsor Arms, and a summer at the Millcroft Inn, I headed to Europe, where I worked in Switzerland—in Gstaad and Davos, and at the Hôtel National in Lucerne, where Escoffier was chef in the early years of the century. We used the same pots Escoffier had used, the same cleavers, the same discipline. Then I was asked by Morden Yolles to come to Toronto to discuss a new restaurant, which turned out to be Scaramouche, where I was partner-chef with Michael Stadtländer from 1979 to 1983. I left to run my own catering business until opening my restaurant, Palmerston, in June 1985.

In discussing my training, I've mentioned organization several times—it's one of the essential things any cook has to learn. Whether you're running a restaurant kitchen that serves seventy people an evening or a home kitchen for four or two or even one, you still need to visualize—to imagine—your meals before you start cooking them. One clue to a meal's success is how close the reality comes to your visualization. Always keep in mind what you want. If it's your five basic food groups (protein, carbohydrates, minerals, vitamins, and fats) in a simple weekday supper, you might try Grilled rib steaks with sautéed potatoes and green beans (p. 63), or any of the other grilled dishes, which are satisfying and easy to prepare, or a Warm salad with lamb and chèvre (p. 40). Weekend evenings are the high-pressure nights in a restaurant—people expect something special, and each night becomes a kind of performance. The same thing is true at home. So for a special dinner party, if you already have some basic skills and want to spend more time cooking, go ahead and make Salmon confit with Pernod and leeks (p. 18). Your guests will enjoy it if you can enjoy making it. Naturally the recipes in this book suit cooks of varying levels of experience. Anyone who's afraid of Salmon confit might take a look at Oysters gratiné (p. 22), which is easier to handle. If you work through the chapter called Base Recipes (pp. 1–16), you will not only ground yourself in some classic techniques but also prepare many of the components required for classic cooking.

For this book I've selected recipes I think are outstanding in their category. While some of them are restaurant-trade oriented, the more elaborate sort of dishes people normally have to go out to eat, others are my version of old standards—Coq au vin (p. 84), Oxtail soup (p. 60), Beef Goulash (p. 68)—which even a new cook should be able to make with a bit of care. In fact, many of the recipes are common-sense interpretations of classical French cuisine, from Navarin of lamb with herb butter (p. 78) to Duck with olives (p. 88), using the best fresh seasonal ingredients available locally. Even the most original recipes, such as Warm salad with calf's liver, apples, and parsley vinaigrette (p. 42), Grouper with curried spinach (p. 92), or Marzipan and apple pastry with warmed sour cherries (p. 126), are thought out in a practical way, so that the ingredients marry well.

You'll notice that almost every recipe concludes with a suggestion about presentation. As long as you've taken the time to prepare a dish, spend the extra minutes to present it in a way that does justice to your efforts. Try serving the main element of the dish surrounded by or on top of the sauce, rather than masked by it (Veal scaloppine with tomato butter, p. 69; Poached pears with caramel sauce, p. 137). This shows off the most important feature and gives color contrast to the dish.

People often ask me what I eat at home. A chef's schedule means late meals after the restaurant closes, so I look forward to nights off, when Cynthia, my wife, shares the cooking with me. We grill outside all year long (except in the worst snowstorms), but some nights what I really want is peanut butter on toast —food doesn't have to be elaborate to be good. Of course styles in food are always changing. As an apprentice I noticed certain trends—the staples in many restaurants were French onion soup, pâté, etc.—and I often thought there must be something more to cooking. The Windsor Arms Hotel made the breakthrough in Toronto in the 1960s, while nouvelle cuisine (the Troisgros brothers, Paul Bocuse, Alain Chapel, to name only a few) made an international impact by emphasizing fresh produce treated simply and arranged beautifully on a plate. These were cooks who wanted freedom of expression, who didn't feel bound to reproduce what Escoffier had done. There's a trend away from nouvelle cuisine now—really a reaction to meals that aren't well thought-out nutritionally, or dishes that combine exotic ingredients without purpose—but it has changed the way we see food, and made us look again at the principles of good cooking that always hold true. If you understand the basics, use the freshest ingredients, and stay flexible in adapting menus and recipes to the market, you'll always make honest, satisfying food.

GLOSSARY

BAIN-MARIE: A hot water bath used as a source of indirect heat for cooking (see Sabayon) or keeping food warm (a double boiler is a kind of bain-marie).

BATONS: Sticks of vegetables or bacon approximately 1½″ (4 cm) long and ¼″ (6 mm) thick.

BLANCH: Literally, to whiten; a preliminary process in which foods are immersed briefly in boiling water (often just until the water returns to the boil); they are usually then refreshed in cold water.

BOUQUET GARNI: A mixture of herbs and vegetables used for flavoring stocks; if they will not be strained out, tie ingredients together to facilitate removal.

BRUNOISE: A mixture of vegetables cut in uniform ⅛″ (3 mm) dice.

CÉLESTINE: A garnish of herb-flavored crêpes cut in julienne.

CHIFFONADE: A garnish of lettuce or other leafy vegetables cut in julienne.

CLARIFICATION: The process of removing impurities from liquids; in the case of consommés, egg whites and flavoring ingredients are boiled up with the liquid to form a raft.

CONCASSÉ (CONCASSER): Literally, to break up; the term is usually applied to tomatoes that have been peeled and seeded and are then roughly chopped—I generally cut them in ½″ (12 mm) squares.

DEGLAZE: To clean out the pan used for roasting or frying by adding liquid (usually wine) and scraping up the brown bits from the bottom; the resulting mixture is the foundation of the sauce of the dish to be prepared.

DEGREASE: To pour off and discard excess fat.

DICE: Small—roughly ⅛″ (3 mm)—cubes.

FILLET (CITRUS FRUIT): A segment from which all skin, membrane, and seeds have been removed.

FUMET: Fish stock, best made from flat saltwater species such as flounder, plaice, or sole (freshwater fish are too oily).

GRATINÉ (GRATINER): To brown with top heat in an oven or under a broiler.

JULIENNE: Fine sticks—usually vegetables—about ⅛″ (3 mm) wide and 2″ (5 cm) long.

LIAISON: A mixture of egg yolks and cream used to bind some sauces (a white wine cream sauce, for instance) and cream soups.

MIREPOIX: A mixture of onion, carrot, and celery cut in uniform ¾″ (2 cm) cubes; used for flavoring basic stocks and sauces.

PRINTANIÈRE: A mixture of vegetables cut in uniform ½″ (12 mm) dice.

PROVIMI: Acronym for the special mixture (protein, vitamins, minerals) usually fed to calves to produce the finest veal.

QUENELLE: An egg-shaped mass made from either a sweet or a savory base; to form quenelles, see p. 117.

RAFT: The mass that floats to the surface of a bouillon during the process of clarification and collects impurities as the liquid percolates through it.

REDUCE: To boil a liquid until most of the moisture evaporates, in order to concentrate the flavor.

REFRESH: To stop the cooking process after blanching by rinsing the food under cold running water or plunging it into cold water until completely cool.

SABAYON: A mixture of egg yolks and flavorings (sweet or savory) beaten over indirect heat to produce a heavy froth with the consistency of a thick mayonnaise.

SAUTÉ (SAUTER): Literally, to jump; to fry quickly, tossing and stirring, in a small amount of oil or butter.

SORBÉTIÈRE: An ice cream or sherbet maker.

TRUSS: To tie the legs and wings close to the body of a fowl as preparation for roasting.

ZEST: The thinly peeled or grated colored outer skin (without any white) of citrus fruit.

BASE RECIPES

Beef bouillon

8 cups (2 L)

2 onions
4 lb beef bones (2 kg)
8 cups cold water (2 L)

Bouquet garni:
2 carrots, 2 stalks celery, 1 leek, all split lengthwise
10 black peppercorns, crushed
2 bay leaves
2 whole cloves
2 sprigs fresh thyme *or* ½ tsp dried (2 mL)

1. Cut onions crosswise in half and blacken on electric element or open gas flame (this adds color to the bouillon).
2. Place bones and water in a stock pot and bring to a boil.
3. Reduce to a simmer and skim surface to remove any scum.
4. Add onions and bouquet garni. Simmer uncovered, without stirring, 5 to 6 hours.
5. Strain liquid through cheesecloth and discard everything else.
6. Use as required or freeze for later use.

Chicken stock

6 cups (1500 mL)

4 lb chicken bones (2 kg)
6 cups cold water (1500 mL)

Bouquet garni:
2 onions, split crosswise
2 carrots, 2 stalks celery, 1 leek, all split lengthwise
10 black peppercorns, crushed
2 bay leaves
2 whole cloves
2 sprigs fresh thyme *or* ½ tsp dried (2 mL)

1. Place bones and water in a stock pot and bring to a boil.
2. Reduce to a simmer and skim surface to remove any scum.
3. Add bouquet garni and simmer, uncovered, 3 to 4 hours.
4. Strain liquid through cheesecloth and discard everything else.
5. Use as required or freeze for later use.

Veal or lamb jus

4 cups (1 L)

3 lb veal *or* lamb bones cut in 1″ to 2″ (2.5- to 5-cm)
    pieces (1.5 kg)
mirepoix of 2 onions, 1 carrot, 1 stalk celery
5 cloves garlic, roughly chopped
½ small tin tomato paste
15 dried juniper berries, crushed
1 sprig fresh thyme *or* ½ tsp dried (2 mL)
3 bay leaves
1 sprig fresh rosemary *or* ½ tsp dried (2 mL)
12 black peppercorns, crushed
1¼ cups red wine (300 mL)

1. Preheat oven to 400°F (200°C).
2. Spread bones in a roasting pan and roast until browned, about 1 hour.
3. Add mirepoix and garlic and continue browning in oven another ½ hour.
4. Add tomato paste and continue browning, stirring frequently, until mixture turns a dark reddish brown, about 20 minutes.
5. Transfer mixture to a stock pot. Add cold water to cover, herbs, and spices and place on high heat.
6. Bring to a boil, reduce to a simmer, and skim surface for scum. Simmer, uncovered, approximately 5 hours.
7. Add wine and continue simmering ½ hour longer.
8. Use as required or freeze for later use.

Fish fumet

6 cups (1500 mL)

2 lb fish bones (preferably from flat saltwater species such
    as turbot, sole, or flounder) (1 kg)
4 cups cold water (1 L)
2 cups white wine (500 mL)

Bouquet garni:
1 stalk celery
1 leek, white only
1 Spanish onion, split crosswise
6 white peppercorns, crushed
1 sprig fresh dill
1 sprig fresh tarragon *or* ¼ tsp dried (1 mL)

1. Place all ingredients in stock pot and bring to a boil.
2. Reduce to a simmer and cook, uncovered, 45 minutes.
3. Strain liquid through cheesecloth and discard everything else.
   (Will keep in refrigerator 2 to 3 days and can be frozen
   indefinitely.)

Special equipment:
Non-oxidizing (stainless steel or enamelled) stock pot (otherwise the fumet will turn cloudy)

Lobster butter

---

approximately 1 lb (450 g)

4 cooked lobster carcasses
1 lb butter (450 g)
1 medium onion, finely chopped
2 cloves garlic, minced
2 leeks, whites only, washed and chopped
¼ tsp caraway seeds (1 g)
1 stalk celery, roughly chopped
⅜ cup white wine (90 mL)
¼ cup cognac (60 mL)
1 cup water (250 mL)

1. Pound lobster carcasses as thoroughly as possible with a meat pounder or mortar and pestle.
2. Melt butter in a large soup pot or casserole. Add onion and garlic and sauté gently 2 minutes.
3. Add leek, caraway, and celery and sauté until golden.
4. Add pounded carcasses and continue sautéing about 15 minutes longer.
5. Deglaze with white wine and cognac.
6. Add water and simmer gently, uncovered, 1 hour, stirring occasionally.
7. Strain liquid into a bowl. Discard vegetables and carcasses.
8. Cover and place in refrigerator to solidify (save the liquid that accumulates in the bottom of the bowl for adding to fish soups, etc.). Lobster butter will keep up to 1 week in refrigerator or indefinitely in freezer; I recommend freezing.

Marinated salmon

approximately 4 lb (2 kg)

4 lb salt (2 kg)
4 lb sugar (2 kg)
1 bunch pickling dill (usually available in late summer) *or*
    regular dill, roughly chopped
equal amount fresh coriander, roughly chopped
1 tsp black peppercorns, crushed (3 g)
1 tbsp coriander seeds, crushed (5 g)
4-lb (2-kg) whole salmon, trimmed and filleted
olive oil to partially cover

1. Combine salt and sugar. Mix in herbs and spices.
2. Sprinkle about one-third of mixture into container.
3. Lay in one salmon fillet, skin side down, and cover completely with another third of mixture.
4. Place second fillet, flesh side down, over first and cover completely with remaining mixture.
5. Cover container with plastic wrap and refrigerate 24 hours, or let rest in a cool place (such as a basement) 12 to 16 hours.
6. Scrape marinade off fillets and put them back in containers. Pour in enough olive oil to partially cover. Cover container and store in refrigerator. (Will keep up to 10 days.)

Special equipment:
Plastic or stainless steel container long enough to hold salmon fillets

Mayonnaise

2 cups (500 mL)

2 egg yolks
1 tbsp Dijon mustard (15 mL)
juice of 1 lemon
¼ cup white wine vinegar (60 mL)
1½ cups vegetable oil (375 mL)
½ cup virgin olive oil (125 mL)
salt and cayenne pepper to taste

1. Combine yolks, mustard, half the lemon juice, and half the vinegar in a stainless steel bowl and whisk briefly.
2. Place bowl on a wet tea towel (to hold it in place), and, whisking constantly, pour in the oils in a steady stream.
3. Approximately halfway through, add remaining vinegar and lemon juice, salt, and cayenne.
4. Add the rest of the oils. If consistency is too thick, whisk in about 1 tablespoon (15 mL) warm water.

Tarragon variation:
Chop 3 sprigs fresh tarragon very finely and add to mayonnaise.

Crème anglaise

6 cups (1500 mL)

4 cups homogenized milk (1 L)
1 cup sugar (250 g)
10 egg yolks
¼ cup cold whipping (35%) cream (60 mL)
1 vanilla bean, split lengthwise and scooped out
2 capfuls pure vanilla extract

1. Combine milk and sugar in a saucepan and scald.
2. Remove from heat and whisk in egg yolks all at once.
3. Return to low heat and stir constantly with a wooden spoon until thickened enough to coat the back of the spoon (about the consistency of house paint).
4. Strain into a mixing bowl.
5. Add cream and vanillas.
6. Use as required or keep in refrigerator up to 1 week.

Vanilla ice cream:
Freeze crème anglaise mixture in a sorbétière.

Crème fraîche

4 cups (1 L)

4 cups whipping (35%) cream (1 L)
juice of 1 lemon
½ cup yogurt (125 mL)

1. Combine all ingredients in a stainless steel bowl.
2. Cover with a clean cloth and leave at room temperature for
   36 hours.
3. Transfer thickened cream to clean glass jars and refrigerate.
   (Will keep in refrigerator 1 week.)

Sweet variation:
Add 3 capfuls pure vanilla extract and ½ cup (125 mL) granulated sugar to mixture before leaving it to sit.

Sugar syrup

4 cups (1 L)

4 cups water (1 L)
2 lb sugar (1 kg)

1. Combine sugar and water in a saucepan and bring to a boil.
2. Cook 5 minutes at a rolling boil.
3. Remove from heat and cool before using.

Meringues

approximately 1 lb (450 g)

5 egg whites
1 tbsp granulated sugar (15 g)
7 tbsp granulated sugar (100 g) combined with ¾ cup
    confectioners' (icing) sugar (100 g)

1. Beat egg whites until stiff peaks form, adding first quantity of sugar halfway through.
2. When stiff, fold in combined sugars.
3. Preheat oven to 200°F (95°C). Line a baking sheet with silicone or parchment paper.
4. Pour mixture into a piping bag and pipe onto lined sheet in the shape of shells roughly 3" (7.5 cm) long and 1" (2.5 cm) wide.
5. Place in oven and prop door open slightly. Leave in warm oven to bake overnight.
6. Cool on a rack for about 20 minutes.
7. Store in a tightly closed tin or plastic bag until ready to use.

Crêpes

18 to 20 8" (20-cm) crêpes

8 eggs
1 ¼ cups all-purpose flour (300 mL)
salt to taste
¼ tsp freshly grated nutmeg (1 mL)
½ cup melted butter (125 g)
4 cups milk (1 L)

1. Combine eggs, flour, salt, and nutmeg. Add melted butter.
2. Add milk and combine well.
3. Let batter rest at least 1 hour before cooking (it should be just thick enough to coat the back of a spoon).
4. Place crêpe pan(s) over medium heat.
5. Grease with butter (after the first crêpes, this step shouldn't be necessary).
6. Ladle in enough batter to coat bottom of pan thinly and cook 2 minutes.
7. Turn and cook 1 minute longer. Slip crêpe onto a wax-papered tray to cool.
8. Use right away or cool thoroughly, stack, and freeze.

Special equipment:
1 or more 8" (20-cm) non-stick crêpe pans

Génoise

9" (22.5-cm) cake

1 cup sugar (250 g)
8 large eggs
grated rind of 1 lemon
⅞ cup unsalted butter (200 g)
2½ cups sifted cake flour (250 g)

1. Preheat oven to 375°F (190°C). Grease and flour a 9" (22.5-cm) springform pan.
2. Combine sugar, eggs, and lemon rind in a stainless steel bowl.
3. Whisk over a simmering bain-marie until frothy and slightly warmer than body temperature.
4. Transfer to another bowl and beat at high speed with an electric mixer until bowl feels cool to the touch.
5. Meanwhile, melt butter and keep warm but not hot.
6. Sift flour and fold into egg mixture with a rubber spatula, scraping sides of bowl.
7. Fold in melted butter (do not overblend, or cake will lose height—you are relying on the beaten eggs for leavening).
8. Pour batter into prepared pan and bake approximately 45 minutes.
9. Cool in pan 1 hour. Turn out and place on a rack until completely cool.
10. Cover with plastic wrap and store in refrigerator up to 1 week (for longer storage, use the freezer).

Chocolate variation:

Follow the above recipe with these changes:

1. Reduce sifted cake flour to 2 cups (200 g) and sift it again with 1⅓ cups (100 g) cocoa powder.
2. Reduce butter to ⅔ cup (150 g).

Choux pastry

approximately 2 lb (1 kg)

1 ¼ cups skim milk (300 mL)
⅔ cup unsalted butter (150 g)
3 cups sifted pastry flour (300 g)
2 ½ tsp salt (15 g)
2 tbsp sugar (30 g)
¼ cup light rum (60 mL)
6 egg yolks

1. Place milk and butter in a saucepan and bring to a boil.
2. Add flour and remove from heat. Then add salt and sugar and blend with a wooden spoon.
3. Return pan to heat and continue beating until dough forms a mass that pulls away from bottom and sides of pan.
4. Place dough in a bowl and beat with an electric mixer on slow speed, adding egg yolks one at a time and waiting until each one is fully absorbed before adding the next.
5. Beat in rum.
6. Cover dough and store in refrigerator until ready to use. (Will keep 1 week.)

Puff pastry

approximately 2 lb (1 kg)

3½ cups all-purpose flour (500 g)
1 cup soft unsalted butter (225 g)
1 tbsp salt (20 g)
⅞ cup cold water (200 mL)
1 cup cold unsalted butter (225 g)

1. Sift flour and cut in first quantity of butter until pieces are no larger than peas.
2. Combine salt and water and add to flour mixture.
3. Knead just until dough is homogeneous—do not overwork.
4. Form into a ball and cross-hatch the top ½″ (12 mm) deep. Cover and refrigerate 1 hour.
5. On a lightly floured surface roll dough into a rectangle about ½″ (12 mm) thick.
6. Pull remaining butter into small pieces and arrange over two-thirds of dough.
7. Beginning with unbuttered end, fold dough into thirds.
8. Turn dough a quarter turn, so the fold is on the bottom, and roll again into a rectangle. Cover and refrigerate ½ hour.
9. Repeat step 8 four more times.
10. Puff pastry is now ready to use. (Will keep in refrigerator only overnight; for longer storage, use freezer.)

Pie pastry

5 lb (2.25 kg)

3 lb (approximately 14 ¼ cups) sifted pastry flour (1360 g)
salt to taste
2 lb cold unsalted butter (900 g)
2 cups cold water (470 mL)
2 tbsp brown sugar (30 mL)

1. Sift flour and salt into a large mixing bowl.
2. Cut butter in small cubes and work into flour by hand until texture resembles that of meal (do not overwork).
3. Add water and sugar all at once and knead by hand until ingredients are well combined (again, do not overwork).
4. Form dough into a log and refrigerate at least 2 hours before rolling.
5. Use as required or freeze in single-use packages.

Sweet pastry

approximately 2 lb (1 kg)

2.2 lb (approximately 10 cups) sifted pastry flour (1 kg)
2⅛ cups unsalted butter (500 g)
3 eggs
1 capful pure vanilla extract
1⅓ cups granulated sugar (300 g)

1. Work flour and butter together as for pie pastry above.
2. Beat together eggs, vanilla, and sugar and add to flour mixture all at once.
3. Work dough until smooth.
4. Refrigerate at least 2 hours before rolling.
5. Use as required or freeze in single-use packages.

APPETIZERS

Salmon confit with Pernod and leeks
Fried potatoes with mascarpone and salmon roe
Shrimp brochettes with fennel and leek
Oysters gratiné
Veal and parsley terrine
Crêpes with foie gras and apple
Toasts with marrow and sea salt
Baked eggs with cheese, cream, and tomato
Poached chèvre with red pepper sauce

Salmon confit with Pernod and leeks

8 portions

2 medium leeks
4 tsp butter (20 g)
4-lb (2-kg) whole salmon, trimmed and filleted
salt and freshly ground pepper to taste
¼ cup Pernod (60 mL)

1. Trim about ¼" (6 mm) from bottom of leeks but leave enough of the root end so that leaves remain attached. Slit in half without cutting through root end and wash well under running water.
2. Blanch in salted boiling water, about 1 minute. Refresh in cold water. Drain and separate leaves.
3. Butter terrine and line it crosswise with overlapping strips of leek, covering bottom and sides completely and leaving strips long enough to hang at least 1" (2.5 cm) over sides.
4. Remove all pin bones from salmon and skin fillets: make an incision near the tail and, with a sawing motion, run knife horizontally under surface of skin without cutting into flesh.
5. Trim fillets to fit exactly into terrine. Reserve trimmings.
6. Place one fillet in terrine skinned side down. Sprinkle with salt, pepper, and one-third of the Pernod.
7. Use trimmings to form a second layer. Sprinkle with more salt, pepper, and Pernod.
8. Top with remaining fillet, skinned side up. Add salt, pepper, and remaining Pernod. Preheat oven to 350°F (180°C).
9. Fold overhanging leek strips over salmon. Use scissors to trim off any long ends.

10. Cover terrine with foil and place in a bain-marie lined with a dish cloth. Add enough hot water to come two-thirds of the way up sides of terrine.
11. Bake 45 minutes, or until a meat thermometer inserted in the center registers 140°F (60°C). Let cool at room temperature.
12. When cool, press under a heavy weight and refrigerate 12 hours. (Will keep in refrigerator about 10 days before cutting.)

Presentation:
Unmold terrine and cut in slices. Serve on cold plates, with Green Salad (p. 31) and Tarragon Mayonnaise (p. 8).

Special equipment:
Aluminum or enamelled cast-iron terrine

A heavy weight for pressing (I recommend two bricks on top of a piece of plywood cut roughly ¼"/6 mm smaller than the terrine)

Fried potatoes with mascarpone and salmon roe

4 portions

4 medium potatoes
2 tbsp butter (25 g)
¾ cup mascarpone (an Italian cream product) (175 mL)
4 oz salmon roe (125 g)
10 fresh chives

1. Boil potatoes in salted water until three-quarters cooked, 10 to 15 minutes. Place in a colander to drain and cool.
2. Peel and slice about ¼" (6 mm) thick.
3. Heat butter in a frying pan until sizzling.
4. Add potatoes and brown carefully on both sides, about 10 minutes.
5. Spread fried potatoes evenly on four warm plates.
6. Dot each portion with several small spoonfuls of mascarpone.
7. Dot each spoonful of mascarpone with salmon roe.
8. Chop chives and sprinkle liberally over top. Serve immediately.

Shrimp brochettes with fennel and leek

4 portions

20 large shrimp
1 bulb fennel
1 medium leek, well washed
4 tsp butter (20 g)
¼ tsp freshly grated nutmeg (1 mL)
¼ cup whipping (35%) cream (50 mL)
salt and freshly ground pepper to taste

1. Light barbecue.
2. Pccl and devein shrimp. Thread onto skewers, piercing each one through both ends.
3. Slice fennel and leek in strips ⅛" (3 mm) thick and 2" (5 cm) long.
4. Heat butter in a frying pan. Add fennel and sauté gently 5 minutes.
5. Add leek and continue sautéing another 5 minutes.
6. Add nutmeg and cream. Taste for salt and pepper.
7. Bring slowly to a boil. Remove from heat and cover to keep warm.
8. Barbecue shrimp approximately 2 minutes on each side. Remove from skewers.

Presentation:
Place a portion of vegetable mixture on each plate and arrange shrimp on top. Serve warm.

Oysters gratiné

2 or 3 portions

Oysters and squash:
1 spaghetti squash
12 fresh oysters (Malpeque or Blue Point)
½ cup brut sparkling white wine (125 mL)
4 tsp butter (20 g)
½ tsp freshly grated nutmeg (2 mL)
1 sprig fresh basil, chopped *or* ¼ tsp dried (1 mL)
salt and freshly ground pepper to taste

Sauce:
poaching liquid from oysters
2 egg yolks
⅔ cup whipping (35%) cream (150 mL)
pinch cayenne pepper

1. Preheat oven to 350°F (180°C).
2. Prick spaghetti squash with a knife tip. Bake approximately 1 hour, or until skin yields to pressure.
3. Shuck oysters and reserve juices.
4. Place oysters in saucepan with juices and wine.
5. Sprinkle a baking tray with rock salt.
6. Rinse bottom half of each oyster shell and place shiny side up on tray (the rock salt will help to steady them).
7. In a large bowl combine butter, nutmeg, basil, salt, and pepper.
8. When squash is done, remove from oven. Scrape out seeds and discard.
9. Scrape flesh from squash into bowl and combine with butter mixture. Using a fork, place some on each oyster shell.

10. Bring oysters to a boil and remove immediately from heat.
11. Place an oyster on each bed of squash.
12. Reduce oyster poaching liquid until it has almost all evaporated.
13. Whisk egg yolks with 2 tbsp (25 mL) of the cream.
14. Add remaining cream to oyster liquid and reduce again until thick. Remove from heat and taste for salt and cayenne. Stir in yolk mixture.
15. Spoon some sauce over each oyster.
16. Preheat broiler.
17. Gratiné oysters under broiler until golden brown (you may have to shift tray around to achieve an even color).

Presentation:
Set each portion of oysters in a bed of rock salt on a small plate.

Special item:
4 to 5 lb good-quality rock salt (2 kg)

Veal and parsley terrine

12 portions

Veal:
2 lb veal bones (1 kg)
2 quarts (approximately) water (2 L)
mirepoix of 1 carrot, 2 stalks celery, 1 large onion
12 peppercorns, crushed
2 whole cloves
2 bay leaves
2 lb trimmed veal shank meat (leave pieces as whole as
    possible) (1 kg)
3 packages gelatin
3 tbsp cold water (45 mL)
salt to taste
2 tbsp cognac (30 mL)
¼ cup white wine (60 mL)

Garnish:
printanière of 2 carrots, 1 white turnip, 1 parsnip
1 bunch Italian parsley, finely chopped
1 sprig fresh thyme, finely chopped
10 black peppercorns, crushed

1. Place veal bones in a large soup pot. Add water to cover and
   bring to a boil.
2. Reduce heat to a simmer and skim surface to remove scum.
3. Add mirepoix, pepper, cloves, and bay leaves and simmer,
   uncovered, 2 hours.
4. Add veal shank meat and continue simmering another 1½
   hours.
5. Remove veal and set aside to cool.
6. Strain stock, discarding bones and mirepoix, and transfer 2
   cups (500 mL) of it to a saucepan (save the rest for another
   use).
7. Soften gelatin with cold water and stir into stock. Taste for
   salt.

8. Add cognac and wine. Keep warm but do not boil.
9. Cut veal in 1" (2.5-cm) cubes and place in a bowl.
10. Add vegetables, parsley, thyme, and peppercorns and mix well.
11. Pack veal-vegetable mixture firmly into terrine—it should come almost to the brim.
12. Pour in warm stock-gelatin mixture and place in refrigerator to set for 4 hours. (Will keep about 10 days.)

Presentation:

Unmold terrine and cut in slices. Serve on cold plates with Mayonnaise (p. 8) and Celery Root Salad (p. 32).

Special equipment:

Aluminum or enamelled cast-iron terrine

Crêpes with foie gras and apple

4 portions

7 oz fresh foie gras (200 g)
2 tbsp cognac (30 mL)
salt and freshly ground pepper to taste
4 Crêpes (p. 12), fresh *or* thawed
2 Spy apples (no substitutes)
¼ cup whipping (35%) cream (50 mL)
2 tbsp butter (25 g)
4 sprigs parsley

1. The day before you plan to serve, marinate foie gras in cognac, salt, and pepper. Cover and refrigerate overnight.
2. If you have frozen crêpes on hand, thaw them; otherwise make fresh ones.
3. Wash and quarter apples (do not peel or core).
4. Put in a small saucepan, cover, and simmer till soft.
5. Pass cooked apples through a strainer. Discard seeds and skins.
6. Preheat oven to 250°F (120°C).
7. Slice marinated foie gras in 4 equal portions.
8. Enclose 1 portion in each crêpe, folding crêpe over once.
9. Place on a baking sheet in oven to warm.
10. Meanwhile, heat apple purée. Beat in cream and butter.

Presentation:
Place a dollop of apple purée in the center of each plate. Lay warm crêpes on top, garnish with parsley sprigs, and serve.

Toasts with marrow and sea salt

2 portions

1 lb marrow bones (beef or veal) (500 g)
2 slices good-quality fresh white bread
coarse sea salt in a grinder

1. Remove marrow by pushing it up through bones and sliding it out.
2. Slice in rounds about ⅛" (3 mm) thick.
3. Toast bread on both sides.
4. Trim off crusts.
5. Arrange marrow slices in overlapping layers on toasts.
6. Place under broiler for about 30 seconds, just until marrow softens and warms slightly.
7. Sprinkle with sea salt and serve right away.

Baked eggs with cheese, cream, and tomato

2 portions

4 tsp soft butter (20 g)
salt and freshly ground pepper to taste
½ clove garlic, pressed to a fine paste
1 sprig fresh oregano
1 tomato, blanched, peeled, seeded, and cut in ½ " (12-mm)
    squares
4 eggs
¼ cup whipping (35%) cream (50 mL)
⅔ cup freshly grated Crotonese *or* Parmesan cheese (50 g)

1. Preheat oven to 350°F (180°C). Butter cocotte dishes.
2. Grind a little salt and pepper into each dish.
3. Rub dishes with garlic paste.
4. Place a few leaves of oregano and one-quarter of the tomato
   pieces in each dish.
5. Break 2 eggs into each dish.
6. Repeat steps 2 and 4.
7. Pour cream on top and sprinkle with grated cheese.
8. Cover dishes with foil or small plates and bake 10 minutes, or
   until eggs are set but not firm.

Presentation:
Serve in dishes with crisp buttered toast points.

Special equipment:
2 cocotte dishes or soufflé molds approximately 3" (7.5 cm) in
diameter

Poached chèvre with red pepper sauce

4 portions

1 large sweet red pepper
2 tsp olive oil (10 mL)
½ clove garlic, mashed
2 tbsp dry white wine (30 mL)
1 head Boston lettuce
5 oz French chèvre (160 g)
2 tbsp cold butter, cubed (25 g)

1. Roast pepper under broiler, turning occasionally, until charred all over, about 15 minutes.
2. Remove from oven and wrap in a clean dish towel to cool and facilitate peeling.
3. When cool, peel off skin and remove seeds. Cut pepper in rough dice.
4. Heat oil in a saucepan and gently sauté pepper and garlic about 10 minutes.
5. Add wine and bring to a boil.
6. Transfer to a food processor or blender and purée.
7. Carefully separate lettuce leaves and choose 7 or 8 of the best, large enough to serve as wrappers for the cheese.
8. Blanch leaves in salted boiling water. Drain and refresh immediately in cold water.
9. Spread carefully, spine side down, on paper towels to drain.
10. Preheat oven to 300°F (150°C).
11. Cut chèvre in 4 equal slices and place in center of lettuce leaves, using extras as required. Fold lettuce around cheese and place packages seam side down on a baking sheet.
12. Place in oven for 5 minutes to warm gently (do not overheat).
13. Meanwhile, reheat pepper purée and whisk in cold butter.

Presentation:
Ladle pools of pepper sauce onto warm plates. Using a spatula, carefully place a chèvre package in the center of each portion. Serve immediately.

SALADS

Green salad
Celery root salad
Hearts of romaine with walnuts
Salade marocaine
New potatoes and green beans in tarragon vinaigrette
Watercress salad with marinated salmon and herb cream
Warm salad with salmon and fennel
Warm salad with lamb and chèvre
Warm salad with calf's liver, apples, and parsley vinaigrette

Green salad

4 portions

Salad:
1 head Belgian endive
½ small head curly endive
½ small head escarole

Dressing:
3 tbsp virgin olive oil (45 mL)
juice of ¼ lemon
2 tbsp white wine vinegar (30 mL)
salt and freshly ground pepper to taste

1. Wash greens in three changes of cool water and break into bite-sized pieces.
2. Dry in a salad dryer (or place in the center of a large tea towel, draw the corners together to make a bag, and swing it around).
3. Place in refrigerator to chill.
4. Place all dressing ingredients in a small bottle and shake vigorously.
5. Transfer chilled greens to a salad bowl and add enough dressing to coat them lightly. Toss gently.

Presentation:
Serve immediately, either as an appetizer or as an accompaniment to a main course such as Grilled Rib Steaks (p. 63).

Celery root salad

12 portions

1 large celery root
½ cup Mayonnaise (p. 8) (125 mL)
salt to taste
juice of ½ lemon

1. Using a scrub brush, wash celery root thoroughly under cold running water.
2. Peel with a paring knife and cut in julienne.
3. Place mayonnaise, salt, and lemon juice in a stainless steel bowl.
4. Add celery root and mix well.

Presentation:
Serve with Veal and Parsley Terrine (p. 24).

Hearts of romaine with walnuts

4 portions

1 head romaine lettuce
¼ cup freshly shelled walnuts (25 g)
juice of ½ lemon
salt and freshly ground pepper to taste
2 tbsp walnut oil (25 mL)
2 tbsp peanut oil (25 mL)

1. Wash lettuce. Separate innermost leaves (the heart) and reserve the rest for another use.
2. Dry heart leaves well and chill them.
3. Pulverize walnuts in a blender, food processor, or nut grinder.
4. Put hearts and ground walnuts in a salad bowl and mix well.
5. Add lemon juice, salt, and pepper.
6. Add oils and toss just enough to coat all the leaves. Serve
   immediately.

Salade marocaine

4 portions

Artichokes:
2 medium globe artichokes
salted water to cover
½ lemon, juiced

Dressing:
3 tbsp olive oil (45 mL)
1 tsp ground cumin (3 g)
1 large shallot, finely chopped
1 clove garlic, pressed
1 egg yolk
2 tsp Dijon mustard (10 mL)
2 tsp lemon juice (10 mL)
2 tsp white wine vinegar (10 mL)
1 small sprig parsley, chopped
salt and freshly ground pepper to taste

Garnish:
1 pint cherry tomatoes, quartered lengthwise
salt and pepper to taste

1. Bring salted water to a boil. Add lemon juice, squeezed lemon half, and artichokes.
2. Reduce heat to a simmer. Cover and cook, turning periodically, 10 to 12 minutes. Remove from heat and let cool in cooking liquid.
3. Put oil for dressing in a saucepan and add cumin. Cook on moderate heat, stirring constantly, until cumin begins to color. Remove from heat and add shallot and garlic.
4. Combine egg yolk with mustard and half of both the lemon juice and the vinegar.

5. Slowly whisk in first the cumin mixture, then remaining lemon juice and vinegar.
6. Add parsley and taste for salt and pepper.
7. Remove outer leaves from artichokes and cut hearts in sixths.
8. Toss cherry tomatoes in salt and pepper.

Presentation:

Place tomatoes in the center of salad plates. Spoon cumin dressing around them and arrange three pieces of artichoke on each portion.

New potatoes and green beans in tarragon vinaigrette

4 portions

12 small new potatoes, scrubbed and eyed
7 oz fresh green beans, as thin as possible (200 g)
1 tbsp Dijon mustard (15 mL)
4 tsp lemon juice (20 mL)
¼ cup vegetable oil (50 mL)
4 tsp tarragon vinegar (20 mL)
¼ cup olive oil (50 mL)
1 small bunch tarragon, chopped
salt and freshly ground pepper to taste

1. Boil potatoes in a large pot of salted water until tender, about 10 minutes. Drain and cool in a colander.
2. Bring another large pot of salted water to a boil and blanch beans, about 3 minutes. Refresh in cold water, hull ends, and drain well.
3. Whisk together mustard, lemon juice, and vegetable oil.
4. Add vinegar, olive oil, and tarragon. Taste for salt and pepper.
5. Slice potatoes, skins on, in ¼" (6-mm) rounds and add to vinaigrette. Keep at room temperature until ready to serve.
6. Just before serving, add green beans.

Presentation:
Serve as a salad with grilled meats.

Watercress salad with marinated salmon and herb cream

4 portions

Herb cream:
¼ cup Mayonnaise (p. 8) (50 mL)
¼ cup Crème Fraîche (p. 10) (50 mL)
1 large leaf spinach
1 small sprig each of coriander, dill, and tarragon, finely
    chopped
juice of ¼ lemon
salt and freshly ground pepper to taste

Salad and salmon:
2 bunches watercress
2 or 3 leaves radicchio
12 thin slices Marinated Salmon (p. 7)

1. Combine mayonnaise and crème fraîche.
2. Chop spinach leaf finely and combine with a few drops of
   water. Transfer to a piece of cheesecloth and wring out juice.
   Add juice to mayonnaise mixture.
3. Add chopped herbs and lemon juice. Taste for salt and pepper.
4. Wash watercress and radicchio. Break off watercress stems
   and tear radicchio in strips.
5. Combine greens, spin dry, and refrigerate.

Presentation:
Place salad in the center of chilled plates and arrange marinated salmon slices on top. Pour herb cream around the rim of
each plate and serve.

Warm salad with salmon and fennel

4 portions

Salad:
1 small head Bibb lettuce
½ small head radicchio rosso
4 bunches mâche (lamb's lettuce)

Salmon and fennel:
½ lb fresh salmon fillet (250 g)
4 tsp butter (20 g)
3 tbsp chopped shallots (20 g)
1 medium bulb fennel

Dressing:
⅓ cup tarragon vinegar (75 mL)
⅓ cup white wine (75 mL)
3 tbsp chopped shallots (20 g)
3 black peppercorns, crushed
¼ cup cold butter, cubed (50 g)
salt and freshly ground pepper to taste

1. Wash salad greens. Dry well and refrigerate.
2. Slice salmon in 8 equal strips and pound slightly.
3. Butter a baking sheet and sprinkle shallots over it.
4. Lay salmon strips over shallots.
5. Dot salmon with remaining butter.
6. Bring vinegar, wine, shallots, and pepper to a boil in a saucepan and reduce until liquid just coats the bottom of pan.
7. Slice fennel bulb in 8 cross-sections. Poach gently in salted water just until tender, about 5 minutes. Preheat broiler.

8. Broil salmon briefly, about 5 minutes. Do not turn. Pour any excess liquid into reduced dressing mixture.
9. Bring reduced mixture back to a boil and whisk in cubed butter. Taste for salt and pepper.

Presentation:

Arrange salad greens on four large dinner plates. Place salmon strips and fennel slices over greens. Pour dressing around rim of each plate and serve immediately.

Warm salad with lamb and chèvre

4 portions

Lamb:
1 cup olive oil (250 mL)
1 clove garlic, crushed
zest of 1 lemon
2 sprigs fresh rosemary *or* ½ tsp dried (2 mL)
coarsely ground black pepper to taste
5 or 6 dried juniper berries, crushed
14 oz boned and trimmed loin *or* leg of lamb (400 g)
salt to taste

Salad:
4 bunches mâche (lamb's lettuce)
1 head Bibb lettuce
3 oz radicchio rosso (100 g)
3 oz curly endive (100 g)
2 tbsp olive oil (25 mL)
juice of ½ lemon

Dressing:
7 oz French chèvre (200 g)
⅓ cup whipping (35%) cream (75 mL)
juice of ½ lemon
freshly ground black pepper to taste

1. The day before you plan to serve, combine olive oil, garlic, lemon zest, rosemary, pepper, and juniper berries. Add lamb and marinate, turning periodically, in refrigerator for 24 hours.
2. Keeping mâche bunches intact, wash all salad greens. Dry well and chill.
3. Grate chèvre for dressing on medium-large holes of grater. Combine with cream, lemon juice, and pepper.
4. Strain lamb marinade and reserve.
5. Cut lamb across the grain in 12 slices and pound flat. Salt and set aside.
6. Skim oil from top of marinade liquid and place in a frying pan (discard the rest). Heat almost to smoking point.
7. Toss salad greens with oil and lemon juice.

Presentation:
Arrange a portion of salad in the center of each plate and pour dressing around the rim. Quickly sauté lamb slices in hot marinade oil (about 10 seconds on each side) and place three on top of each salad. Serve immediately.

Warm salad with calf's liver, apples, and parsley vinaigrette

2 portions

Salad:
1 small head Bibb lettuce
equal quantity young spinach leaves

Liver and apples:
6 oz calf's liver (180 g)
1 small Spy apple
1 medium shallot (15 g)
4 tsp butter (20 g)
salt and freshly ground pepper to taste

Vinaigrette:
1 tbsp Dijon mustard (15 mL)
4 tsp apple cider (20 mL)
2 tbsp red wine vinegar (25 mL)
2 tsp olive oil (10 mL)
¼ cup chopped parsley (10 g)
2 tsp butter (10 g)

1. Wash lettuce and spinach. (Use several changes of water for the spinach.) Dry well and chill.
2. Cut liver in 6 thin slices approximately 2″ (5 cm) long.
3. Peel, core, and slice apple about ¼″ (6 mm) thick.
4. Peel and slice shallots.
5. Arrange salad greens on plates.
6. Heat butter in a large skillet.

7. Gently sauté apples and shallots about 5 minutes.
8. Push to one side and add liver. Sauté briefly (the inside should still be pink). Add salt and pepper to taste after cooking.
9. Arrange apples, shallots, and liver over salad greens.
10. Return pan to medium heat. Add mustard, cider, vinegar, oil, and parsley.
11. Whisk in butter.

Presentation:
Pour warm dressing over salad and serve immediately.

SOUPS

Cream of tomato with basil
Cauliflower purée with fresh salmon
New potato purée with dill and salmon roe
Fresh green pea purée with prosciutto
Potato and turnip purée with thyme and parsley
Vegetable soup with orange zest and saffron
Essence of chanterelles with fresh thyme célestine
Tomato consommé with vegetable brunoise and basil
Beef consommé with marrow and vegetable brunoise
Capon consommé with ginger and lemon
Mussel and clam soup with spinach and tomato
Green soup with scallops
Oxtail soup

Cream of tomato with basil

6 portions

Clarification:
2 lb fresh ripe tomatoes (1 kg)
⅔ cup fresh basil leaves (30 g)
1 small onion
3 cloves garlic
1½ strips bacon (40 g)
¼ cup olive oil (50 mL)
¼ cup butter (50 g)
½ cup whipping (35%) cream (125 mL)
¼ tsp black peppercorns, crushed (1 g)
salt to taste

Garnish:
¼ cup whipping (35%) cream (50 mL)
finely sliced fresh basil (optional)

1. Chop tomatoes coarsely. Mince basil.
2. Peel and chop onion and garlic.
3. Dice bacon in fine pieces.
4. Place a large saucepan or soup pot on medium heat. Add oil and butter.
5. Gently sauté onion, garlic, and bacon 5 minutes.
6. Add tomatoes, bring to a boil, and simmer 10 minutes.
7. Purée tomato mixture with an immersion blender or in a food processor. Pass through a strainer back into pan.
8. Place on medium heat. Stir in cream, minced basil, and pepper. Taste for salt.
9. Whip cream for garnish.

Presentation:
Ladle soup into warm cups or bowls. Garnish with a swirl of whipped cream and the optional sliced basil.

Cauliflower purée with fresh salmon

6 portions

Soup:
2 tbsp butter (25 g)
1 slice bacon, cut in fine dice (25 g)
5 or 6 caraway seeds
1 medium cauliflower, broken in small flowerets (discard stem)
3 cups Chicken Stock (p. 3) (750 mL)
juice of 1 lemon
2 egg yolks
½ cup whipping (35%) cream (125 mL)
salt and freshly ground pepper to taste

Garnish:
6 oz fresh salmon fillet (180 g)
1 sprig fresh coriander

1. Melt butter and gently sauté bacon 5 minutes.
2. Add caraway seeds and cauliflower pieces.
3. Pour in chicken stock to cover and add lemon juice.
4. Bring to a boil and continue boiling, uncovered, 2 minutes.
5. Purée in blender or food processor and pass through a sieve back into pot.
6. Whisk egg yolks with cream and stir into soup.
7. Heat soup through but do not allow it to boil.
8. Remove from heat and taste for salt and pepper.
9. Cut salmon fillet in 6 strips and pound very flat with the broad side of a knife or cleaver.

Presentation:
Ladle soup into warm bowls. Place a piece of pounded raw salmon on top of each portion, with a leaf or two of coriander beside it.

New potato purée with dill and salmon roe

6 portions

Soup:
1 medium onion
1½ lb new potatoes (750 g)
1 small celery root
⅓ cup butter (75 g)
6 cups Chicken Stock (p. 3) (1500 mL)
3 tbsp tarragon vinegar (45 mL)
1 cup whipping (35%) cream (250 mL)
1 small bunch dill, finely chopped
salt and freshly ground pepper to taste

Garnish:
1 oz salmon roe (30 g)
6 small sprigs dill
¼ cup whipping (35%) cream (50 mL)

1. Peel and dice onion, potatoes, and celery root.
2. Melt butter in a large soup pot. Add diced vegetables and sauté gently 5 minutes.
3. Add stock and vinegar and bring to a simmer. Simmer, uncovered, ½ hour.
4. Purée in blender or food processor and pass through a sieve back into pot.
5. Bring to a boil and add cream.
6. Return to a boil and add dill. (Soup should be thick, but not too thick—add more cream if necessary).
7. Taste for salt and pepper.
8. Whip cream for garnish.

Presentation:
Ladle soup into warm bowls. Place a dollop of whipped cream in the center of each portion and garnish with a dab of salmon roe and a sprig of dill. Serve immediately.

Fresh green pea purée with prosciutto

6 portions

1 large Spanish onion, sliced
1 medium leek, washed and diced
2 slices bacon, finely chopped
½ cup butter (125 g)
2 medium new potatoes, peeled and diced
4 cups Chicken Stock (p. 3) (1 L)
1 lb freshly shelled green peas (500 g)
¾ cup whipping (35%) cream (175 mL)
¼ lb prosciutto, cut in julienne (125 g)

1. Gently sauté onion, leek, and bacon in butter 5 minutes.
2. Add potatoes and continue sautéing 5 minutes longer.
3. Add stock and cook until potatoes are nearly tender, about 25 minutes.
4. Add peas and cook 5 minutes longer.
5. Purée in a blender or food processor and pass through a sieve back into pot.
6. Add cream and heat through.

Presentation:
Ladle into warm soup plates and garnish each portion with a sprinkling of prosciutto.

Potato and turnip purée with thyme and parsley

6 portions

1 medium Spanish onion
½ lb white turnips (250 g)
1 lb potatoes (500 g)
¼ cup butter (50 g)
6 cups Chicken Stock (p. 3) (1500 mL)
⅓ cup chopped parsley (25 g)
1 sprig fresh thyme
½ cup whipping (35%) cream (125 mL)
1 tbsp balsamic vinegar (15 mL)
salt and freshly ground pepper to taste
2 tbsp sour cream (30 mL)

1. Peel and dice onion, turnips, and potatoes.
2. Melt butter in a large soup pot and gently sauté onion and turnip about 10 minutes.
3. Add potatoes and chicken stock and cook gently about 1 hour.
4. Purée in a food processor or with an immersion blender.
5. Return purée to pot and bring to a boil. Add parsley, thyme, cream, and vinegar.
6. Taste for salt and pepper.

Presentation:
Ladle soup into warm bowls and garnish each serving with a dollop of sour cream.

Vegetable soup with orange zest and saffron

6 portions

Soup:
mirepoix of 1 small celery root, 1 carrot, 1 onion, 1 leek
    (white only)
1 large potato, peeled and roughly diced
1 clove garlic, chopped
2 tbsp butter (25 g)
1 tbsp olive oil (15 mL)
zest of 2 oranges
½ phial saffron infused in ½ cup white wine (125 mL)
6 cups Chicken Stock (p. 3) (1500 mL)
1 whole clove
1 sprig thyme
1 bay leaf
2 egg yolks
1 cup whipping (35%) cream (250 mL)

Garnish:
brunoise of ½ stalk celery, ½ carrot, 1 small potato,
    ½ leek
¼ cup whipping (35%) cream (50 mL)
6 strands saffron

1. Blanch brunoise for garnish. Refresh in cold water, drain, and set aside.
2. In a heavy-bottomed soup pot, gently sauté all soup vegetables in butter and oil 10 minutes.
3. Add orange zest, saffron infusion, stock, clove, thyme, and bay leaf and simmer 1 hour.

4. Purée mixture in a blender or food processor and pass through a sieve back into pot.
5. Whisk together egg yolks and cream.
6. Add to soup and heat through (do not boil).
7. Whip cream for garnish.

Presentation:

Place a portion of brunoise in each bowl and ladle in the soup. Float a spoonful of whipped cream on the surface and garnish with a strand of saffron.

Essence of chanterelles with fresh thyme célestine

6 portions

Clarification:
1 lb fresh chanterelles (500 g)
1 medium onion
2 cloves garlic
1 leek, well-washed
1 stalk celery
½ tsp freshly grated nutmeg (2 mL)
3 egg whites
1 recipe cold Beef Consommé (p. 54)
salt to taste

Garnish:
1 recipe Crêpe batter (p. 12)
2 sprigs fresh thyme, chopped *or* ½ tsp dried (2 mL)
3 to 6 whole chanterelles

1. Roughly chop all clarification vegetables.
2. Place in a large soup pot with nutmeg and egg whites and mix well.
3. Add cold consommé and, stirring periodically, bring to a boil.
4. When raft forms, reduce heat and simmer 1½ hours.
5. Meanwhile, make crêpe batter. Add chopped thyme and let sit ½ hour.
6. Cook crêpes and place on a tray (in a single layer) to cool.
7. When cool, slice in fine julienne (célestine), allowing about 1 tbsp (15 mL) per portion. (Stack and freeze remaining crêpes for another time.)
8. Strain consommé and taste for salt.

Presentation:
Place garnish in warm soup bowls. Ladle in hot consommé.

Tomato consommé with vegetable brunoise and basil

6 portions

Clarification:
4 lb very ripe tomatoes (2 kg)
3 cloves garlic
1 carrot
1 leek, well washed
1 small celery heart *or* 2 stalks
12 leaves fresh basil *or* 1 tbsp dried (15 mL)
1 tsp freshly grated nutmeg (5 mL)
4 egg whites
salt to taste
10 grinds black pepper

Garnish:
brunoise of ¼ leek, ½ carrot, ½ stalk celery, 1 tomato
chiffonade of 1 sprig fresh basil

1. Coarsely chop tomatoes, garlic, carrot, leek, celery, and basil.
2. Process vegetables approximately 5 seconds in food processor with steel blade (or dice in small pieces).
3. Transfer to a large, heavy-bottomed soup pot.
4. Add nutmeg, egg whites, salt, and pepper and bring quickly to a boil.
5. When raft forms, reduce heat and simmer 2 hours.
6. Meanwhile, cut and blanch vegetables for brunoise garnish and cut chiffonade of basil.
7. After 2 hours, strain consommé through cheesecloth into a clean pot.

Presentation:
Place a heaping tablespoon (15 mL) of garnish in the bottom of each soup bowl. Bring strained consommé to a boil and ladle into bowls. (You can also serve this consommé chilled.)

Beef consommé with marrow and vegetable brunoise

6 portions

Clarification:
1 Spanish onion
1 leek
½ celery root
1 medium carrot
1 clove garlic
2 lb beef shank meat (1 kg)
1 sprig fresh thyme
2 bay leaves
2 whole cloves
1½ tsp black peppercorns, crushed (5 g)
1 whole nutmeg, grated
1 tbsp tomato paste (15 mL)
2 egg whites
salt to taste
8 cups Beef Bouillon (p. 2) *or* water (2 L)

Garnish:
6 slices beef marrow
brunoise of ½ carrot, ¼ celery root, ½ leek

1. Clean, peel, and coarsely chop onion, leek, celery root, carrot, and garlic.
2. Process to rough dice in a food processor with metal blade (or chop by hand). Transfer to a large, heavy-bottomed soup pot.
3. Cut shank meat in stew-sized pieces.
4. Process in food processor until ground (not too finely).
5. Combine ground shank with vegetables.
6. Add remaining ingredients and mix well.
7. Add bouillon or water and bring to a boil, stirring often.

8. Reduce heat and simmer 2 hours.
9. Meanwhile, cut and blanch vegetables for brunoise garnish.
10. Strain consommé through cheesecloth into a clean pot.

Presentation:

Warm soup bowls in oven. In each bowl place a portion of brunoise and a slice of marrow. Bring strained consommé to a boil, ladle into bowls, and serve.

Capon consommé with ginger and lemon

6 portions

Clarification:
legs of a 6-lb (3-kg) capon *or* boiling fowl
mirepoix of 2 medium onions, 1 medium carrot, 1 medium
    leek, ½ stalk celery
1 clove garlic, chopped
zest and juice of 1 lemon
2 tbsp chopped fresh ginger (15 g)
2 egg whites
10 black peppercorns, crushed
½ tsp freshly grated nutmeg (2 mL)
salt to taste
1 whole clove
2 bay leaves
1 small sprig fresh thyme

Garnish:
1″ (2.5-cm) piece fresh ginger
1 lemon

1. Bone capon legs and cut meat in brunoise.
2. Place meat and mirepoix in a large soup pot. Add all remaining clarification ingredients and mix well.
3. Add cold water to cover. Stirring periodically, bring to a boil.
4. When raft forms, reduce heat and simmer 1½ hours.
5. Meanwhile, peel ginger and cut in fine julienne.
6. Peel lemon and separate fillets. Cut in small pieces.
7. Strain simmered consommé into a clean pot through a sieve lined with cheesecloth.
8. Bring back to a boil. Taste for salt and pepper.

Presentation:
Place ginger julienne and lemon pieces in warm soup plates. Ladle in hot consommé and serve immediately.

Mussel and clam soup with spinach and tomato

4 portions

Soup:
20 medium mussels (evenly sized)
12 small littleneck clams
2 tbsp olive oil (30 mL)
2 shallots, chopped
1 clove garlic, chopped
1 cup white wine (250 mL)
1 tbsp Pernod (15 mL)
2 tbsp cold butter, cubed (30 g)

Garnish:
1 small sprig parsley, chopped
1 small sprig thyme, chopped
1 tomato, blanched, peeled, seeded, and cut in julienne
3 leaves fresh spinach, cut in chiffonade

1. Clean and beard mussels. Rinse clams.
2. Heat oil in a saucepan and gently sauté shallots and garlic about 5 minutes.
3. Add clams and wine. Cover and steam about 5 minutes.
4. When clams begin opening, add mussels. Cover and steam another 5 minutes.
5. When all have opened, transfer mussels and clams to warm soup bowls, dividing portions equally.
6. Bring broth back to a boil. Whisk in Pernod and butter.
7. Stir in all garnish ingredients.

Presentation:
Pour broth evenly over the four portions of shellfish and serve immediately.

Green soup with scallops

6 portions

Soup:
¼ cup butter (50 g)
1 medium onion, chopped
¾ lb new potatoes, peeled and sliced ¼" (6 mm) thick
    (350 g)
3 cups Fish Fumet (p. 5) (750 mL)
1 leek, white only, washed and diced
1 bunch broccoli, heads only, broken in small flowerets
1 bunch fresh coriander, finely chopped (about
    ¼ cup/50 mL)
½ bunch Italian parsley, finely chopped (about
    ½ cup/125 mL)
1 small bunch fresh tarragon, finely chopped (about
    2 tbsp/25 mL)
1 cup white wine (250 mL)
2 egg yolks
½ cup whipping (35%) cream (125 mL)
4 tsp Pernod (20 mL)

Garnish:
½ lb fresh sea scallops (250 g)

1. Melt butter in a large soup pot and add chopped onion. Sauté gently 5 minutes.
2. Add potatoes and fish fumet. Bring to a boil.
3. Add diced leek and cook 5 minutes.
4. Add broccoli flowerets. Bring back to a boil and remove from heat.
5. Purée in blender or food processor and pass through a sieve back into pot.
6. Add chopped herbs and wine.

7. Whisk egg yolks with cream and stir into soup.
8. Add Pernod and gently reheat soup (do not allow it to boil).
9. Slice scallops ¼" (6 mm) thick and pound paper-thin with the broad side of a knife or cleaver.

Presentation:
Ladle soup into warm bowls and garnish each portion with raw scallop slices.

Oxtail soup

6 portions

2 tbsp vegetable oil (25 mL)
1¾-lb oxtail, cut in 1″ (2.5-cm) pieces (800 g)
brunoise of 2 medium onions, 2 medium carrots, 1 small
    celery root, 2 medium parsnips, 2 medium potatoes
1 clove garlic, chopped
½ small tin tomato paste
1 bay leaf
5 or 6 caraway seeds
1 small sprig thyme
10 black peppercorns, crushed
1 whole clove
salt and freshly ground pepper to taste

1. Heat oil in a heavy-bottomed soup pot.
2. Add oxtail pieces and sear on both sides. Remove from pot.
3. Add brunoise and garlic and sauté gently 10 minutes.
4. When vegetables begin to brown, add tomato paste and continue sautéing, stirring constantly, until it turns a deep reddish brown, 7 to 10 minutes.
5. Add seared oxtail pieces, bay leaf, caraway, thyme, pepper, clove, and water to cover. Cover pot and simmer 2 hours.
6. After 2 hours, remove oxtail pieces and take meat from bones.
7. Cut meat as for brunoise and return to soup.
8. Bring to a boil and taste for salt and pepper.

Presentation:
Serve piping hot in soup bowls.

MAIN COURSES: MEATS

Raw beef tenderloin with shallots and mustard sauce
Grilled rib steaks with sautéed potatoes and green beans
Boiled beef with vegetables and horseradish sauce
Salad with marinated raw beef and chanterelles
Beef goulash
Veal scaloppine with tomato butter
Veal with vermouth and rosemary glaze
Roast rack of veal with caramelized shallots
Ossobuco with lemon and marrow
Veal kidney with mustard and vinegar
Calf's liver with rösti potatoes and caramelized onions
Kassler with asparagus and warm potato salad
Pork chops with mushrooms and apple purée
Navarin of lamb with herb butter
Loin of lamb with leeks

Raw beef tenderloin with shallots and mustard sauce

2 portions

Beef and shallots:
2 tbsp red wine (25 mL)
2 tbsp red wine vinegar (25 mL)
4 shallots, very finely chopped
4 oz beef tenderloin (125 g)

Sauce:
1 egg yolk
1 tbsp Dijon mustard (15 mL)
1 tbsp tarragon vinegar (15 mL)
1 tbsp whipping (35%) cream (15 mL)

1. Combine wine, vinegar, and shallots and set aside to marinate.
2. Cut tenderloin in approximately 6 thin slices and pound until very thin.
3. Place egg yolk in a stainless steel bowl and add mustard and vinegar.
4. Whisk over a simmering bain-marie until thickened to the consistency of mayonnaise, 2 to 3 minutes.
5. Stir in cream.

Presentation:
Spoon marinated shallots generously onto two plates. Arrange sliced tenderloin on top and sprinkle with some of the marinade. Pour mustard sauce evenly around beef and serve.

Grilled rib steaks with sautéed potatoes and green beans

2 portions

Steaks:
2 tbsp Dijon mustard (30 mL)
1 clove garlic, chopped
1½ " (4-cm) stem fresh rosemary, roughly chopped *or* ½ tsp
    dried (2 mL)
salt and freshly ground pepper to taste
2 ½ -lb (250-g) rib steaks

Potatoes and beans:
3 or 4 new potatoes, skins on
2 tbsp butter (30 g)
salt to taste
4 oz green beans (125 g)
4 tsp butter (20 g)

1. Light barbecue (optional: steaks may also be pan-fried).
2. Combine mustard, garlic, rosemary, salt, and pepper. Rub
   into steaks and set aside.
3. Boil potatoes in salted water until three-quarters cooked.
   Drain and cool in a colander. When cool, peel and slice ¼"
   (6 mm) thick.
4. Blanch beans in salted water, about 3 minutes, and refresh.
   Hull ends.
5. Melt butter for potatoes in a large, heavy saucepan. Sauté
   slices until golden on both sides. Season with salt.
6. Add beans and additional butter. Reduce heat and simmer
   about 4 minutes. Taste for salt and keep warm.
7. Grill or pan-fry steaks to desired degree of doneness.

Presentation:
Spread vegetables over plates. When steaks are ready, place on
top of vegetables and serve.

Boiled beef with vegetables and horseradish sauce

6 portions

Beef and vegetables:
2 lb beef bones (1 kg)
mirepoix of 1 leek, 1 onion, 1 carrot, 1 stalk celery
2 bay leaves
1 tbsp fresh thyme leaves (15 mL)
1 whole clove
12 or 14 peppercorns, crushed
salt to taste
3 medium potatoes
1 small turnip
2 medium parsnips
1 leek
3-lb (1.5-kg) brisket point

Sauce:
1 cup whipping (35%) cream (250 mL)
⅔ cup freshly grated horseradish (50 g)
salt, pepper, and freshly grated nutmeg to taste
5 leaves fresh spinach, finely chopped

1. Place beef bones, mirepoix, herbs, and spices in a large soup pot with water to cover and bring to a boil. Reduce heat and simmer, uncovered, 2 hours, periodically skimming off scum.
2. Meanwhile, peel and quarter potatoes. Peel turnip and cut in matchsticks. Peel parsnips and cut lengthwise in sixths. Cut leek lengthwise in half and wash well, then cut halves lengthwise in thirds.
3. After 2 hours' simmering, add brisket to bouillon and continue simmering approximately 2 hours. Twenty minutes before the end of cooking, ladle out ½ cup (125 mL) of bouillon for the sauce and start adding the vegetables, potatoes first.

4. After 12 minutes, add turnip and parsnips. Cook 5 minutes longer, then add leek for the last 3 minutes.
5. Meanwhile, reduce reserved bouillon by half. Add cream and reduce again by half. Add horseradish and taste for salt, pepper, and nutmeg.
6. Following the directions on p. 37 (step 2), squeeze juice from chopped spinach leaves and add it to sauce.

Presentation:

Arrange vegetables on a large serving platter. Slice beef across the grain and place in the center. Pour some of the bouillon over the meat and vegetables and serve the sauce separately.

Salad with marinated raw beef and chanterelles

2 portions

Beef:
1 shallot, finely chopped
½ cup dry red wine (125 mL)
1 small sprig fresh thyme, chopped
salt and freshly ground pepper to taste
2 tbsp virgin olive oil (30 mL)
6 oz beef tenderloin, in one piece (180 g)

Salad:
2 leaves curly endive
6 leaves Belgian endive
2 leaves radicchio rosso
1 tbsp grated fresh horseradish (5 g) *or* 1 tsp prepared
    (5 mL)
salt to taste
1 tbsp olive oil (15 mL)

Chanterelles:
4 oz chanterelles (125 g)
¼ cup finely diced bacon (30 g)
1 shallot, chopped
2 tbsp butter (30 g)
1 small sprig parsley, chopped
1 small sprig fresh thyme, chopped
1 tbsp tarragon vinegar (15 mL)

1. Combine all ingredients for beef marinade.
2. Wash and dry salad greens. Refrigerate.
3. Combine horseradish, salt, and oil for dressing.
4. Clean chanterelles by floating them in three changes of
   water. Dry well on paper towels.
5. Slice large chanterelles (leave small ones whole).

6. Slice beef in 6 pieces and pound very thin. (Do not put in marinade yet, or it will discolor.)
7. Sauté bacon and shallot in butter about 3 minutes.
8. Add chanterelles, parsley, and thyme, and continue sautéing another 5 minutes.
9. Add vinegar and taste for salt. Set aside.
10. Toss salad greens with dressing.
11. Dip beef quickly in marinade.

Presentation:
Mound salad greens in the center of two large plates. Drape beef slices on top and drizzle with marinade. Spoon sautéed chanterelles around salads and serve.

Beef goulash

---

6 portions

2 lb stewing beef cut in 1″ (2.5-cm) cubes (1 kg)
1 ½ lb Spanish onions cut in ⅛″ (3-mm) rings (750 g)
salt and freshly ground pepper to taste
¼ cup Hungarian paprika (60 mL)
¼ cup vegetable oil (60 mL)
½ small tin tomato paste
2 whole cloves
2 bay leaves
½ bunch Italian parsley
½ tsp caraway seeds (2 mL)
3 cloves garlic
zest of 2 lemons

1. Combine beef and onions and season with salt, pepper, and paprika.
2. Heat oil in a large stewing pot or Dutch oven to just below smoking point.
3. Add beef and onions and wait 5 minutes before stirring.
4. Stir around and then sear, undisturbed, 5 minutes longer.
5. Add tomato paste and reduce heat slightly. Stir more often now until mixture is an even brown color, about 10 minutes.
6. Add just enough water to cover. Bring to the boil and add cloves and bay leaves.
7. Reduce to a simmer, cover, and stew 2 hours.
8. Meanwhile, chop together parsley, caraway, garlic, and lemon zest until almost paste consistency.
9. Add mixture to stew 15 minutes before end of cooking time.
10. Taste for salt and serve immediately with potatoes or noodles.

Veal scaloppine with tomato butter

2 portions

½ lb provimi veal from inside round of leg (250 g)
2 eggs
1⅓ cups freshly grated Parmesan cheese (100 g)
2 ripe medium tomatoes
1 sprig fresh basil, chopped *or* ¼ tsp dried (1 mL)
salt and freshly ground pepper to taste
2½ tbsp cold butter, cubed (35 g)
2 tbsp olive oil (30 mL)
flour for dredging
2 sprigs fresh basil

1. Cut veal in 6 pieces and pound quite flat.
2. Lightly beat eggs and combine with Parmesan.
3. Blanch tomatoes. Peel, seed, and chop roughly.
4. Place tomatoes in a small saucepan with basil, salt, and pepper and set over moderate heat to warm. When simmering, whisk in butter.
5. Heat oil in a large skillet.
6. Dredge scaloppine in flour and dip in egg mixture.
7. Fry in oil 2 minutes on each side, or until golden.

Presentation:
Just before scaloppine are done, spoon a pool of tomato butter onto each plate. Transfer cooked scaloppine directly to plates. Garnish with sprigs of basil and serve immediately.

Veal with vermouth and rosemary glaze

4 portions

1 lb provimi veal (500 g)
salt and freshly ground pepper to taste
3″ (7.5-cm) stem fresh rosemary *or* 1 tsp dried (5 mL)
¼ cup olive oil (50 mL)
⅜ cup dry vermouth (90 mL)
2 tbsp cold butter (30 g)
1 small sprig fresh rosemary, chopped

1. Cut veal across the grain in 12 equal slices.
2. Between two layers of waxed paper, pound slices with a meat pounder (or the bottom of a heavy saucepan) until quite thin.
3. Season slices with salt, pepper, and rosemary.
4. In a heavy-bottomed skillet, heat oil almost to the smoking point.
5. Sauté veal slices 10 seconds on each side and place directly on warm plates.
6. Discard oil from skillet. If pan is too hot—it probably will be—turn off heat at this point. Deglaze pan with vermouth, stirring with a wire whisk, until liquid is reduced to a syrupy consistency.
7. Add cold butter and rosemary to glaze, whisking vigorously. If pan has started to cool, turn on heat to low. After all butter is incorporated, glaze should come to the boiling point.
8. Pour glaze over veal and serve immediately.

Roast rack of veal with caramelized shallots

6 portions

7 shallots, finely chopped
1 cup red wine (250 mL)
4-rib veal rack, trimmed
1 clove garlic, minced *or* pressed
1 sprig fresh oregano, chopped
salt and freshly ground pepper to taste
2 tbsp red wine (30 mL)
2 tbsp cold butter, cubed (30 g)

1. Put shallots in a saucepan with red wine and bring to a boil. Reduce heat and simmer ½ hour, until most of the liquid has evaporated.
2. Meanwhile, rub veal rack with garlic, oregano, salt, and pepper.
3. Preheat oven to 400°F (200°C). Place veal rack in roasting pan, fat side up.
4. Roast 15 minutes, then reduce heat to 375°F (190°C). Turn rack fat side down and continue roasting approximately 40 minutes longer.
5. Remove from oven and let rest 10 to 15 minutes, then cut in thick slices.
6. Deglaze pan with the 2 tbsp (30 mL) red wine. Add shallot mixture and whisk in cold butter.

Presentation:
Spoon shallot mixture around the outside of individual plates. Place veal slices in the center and serve.

Ossobuco with lemon and marrow

4 portions

1 lb marrow bones (500 g)
4 pieces veal shank (equal thickness)
salt and pepper to taste
2 tbsp olive oil (25 mL)
mirepoix of 1 carrot, 1 stalk celery, 1 medium onion
1 overripe tomato, chopped
1 cup red wine (250 mL)
2 cups Veal Jus (p. 4) (500 mL)
1 bay leaf
6 peppercorns
1 small sprig thyme
1 parsnip
1 carrot
1 leek, well washed
1 small celery root
1 onion
1 lemon
2 tbsp cold butter, cubed (25 g)

1. Remove marrow from bones and chop very finely.
2. Season shanks with salt and pepper.
3. Heat oil in a large casserole and sear shanks until brown on both sides. Remove from pan.
4. Brown mirepoix in same pan, over medium heat, about 10 minutes.
5. Add chopped tomato and continue browning, stirring frequently, until it turns a dark reddish-brown.
6. Pour off excess fat and add wine.
7. Reduce liquid until syrupy (about 5 minutes' steady boiling).
8. Add veal jus, bay leaf, peppercorns, and thyme.
9. Return shanks to pan; liquid should just cover them. Reduce heat, cover, and simmer 45 minutes.

10. Meanwhile, cut vegetables in printanière.
11. Blanch in salted boiling water. Drain and refresh in cold water.
12. Peel lemon. Remove fillets and dice them.
13. Test to see if shanks are done—the meat should pull away slightly from the bone. If necessary, cook another 15 minutes and test again.
14. When done, transfer shanks to a warm serving dish. Strain liquid, discarding mirepoix, and reduce by half.
15. Beat cold butter and chopped marrow into liquid with a wire whisk. Add blanched vegetables and diced lemon.

Presentation:

Ladle sauce and vegetables onto warm plates. Place a veal shank in the center of each portion and serve immediately, with Spätzle (p. 105).

Veal kidney with mustard and vinegar

2 portions

7 oz absolutely fresh veal kidney (200 g)
1 tbsp butter (15 g)
2 tbsp seed mustard (30 mL)
1 tbsp balsamic vinegar (15 mL)
2 tbsp white wine (30 mL)
1 tbsp Veal Jus (p. 4) (15 mL)
2 tbsp whipping (35%) cream (30 mL)
salt and freshly ground pepper to taste

1. Slice kidney into medallions the size of silver dollars and ¼" (6 mm) thick.
2. Remove excess fat.
3. Heat butter in a frying pan and sauté medallions 1 minute on each side. Transfer to a warm plate.
4. Add mustard to pan and sauté about 30 seconds.
5. Deglaze with vinegar, wine, and veal jus. Increase heat and reduce liquid by half.
6. Add cream and reduce again to sauce consistency. Taste for salt and pepper.
7. At the last minute, fold in medallions.

Presentation:
Serve immediately with pasta or potatoes.

Calf's liver with rösti potatoes and caramelized onions

4 portions

5 medium potatoes, skins on
2 medium onions, finely sliced
½ cup butter (125 g)
½ cup Veal Jus (p. 4) (125 mL)
¼ cup beer (50 mL)
salt and freshly ground pepper to taste
1 ½ strips bacon, finely chopped (40 g)
2 tbsp vegetable oil (30 mL)
14 oz calf's liver, cut in 8 thin slices (400 g)

1. Boil potatoes until three-quarters cooked. Drain and cool in a colander.
2. Gently sauté onions in one-quarter of the butter, stirring frequently, until thoroughly caramelized but not burnt, about ½ hour.
3. Add veal jus and beer and simmer 5 minutes. Taste for salt and pepper.
4. Meanwhile, peel potatoes and grate in medium shreds.
5. Heat a non-stick frying pan and add one-quarter of the remaining butter.
6. Add one-quarter of the bacon and one-quarter of the potatoes.
7. Form into a flat pancake and brown over medium-low heat, about 10 minutes on each side. Place on a plate in a 225°F (110°C) oven to keep warm.
8. Make three more pancakes, placing each one in oven on a separate plate.
9. Heat oil in a large skillet and quickly sauté liver slices (about 20 seconds on each side, or to taste).

Presentation:
Arrange liver slices over rösti. Spoon onion sauce around and on top. Serve immediately.

Kassler with asparagus and warm potato salad

4 portions

4 medium potatoes, skins on
2 egg yolks
2 tbsp Dijon mustard (30 mL)
1 tbsp tarragon vinegar (15 mL)
¾ cup vegetable oil (175 mL)
salt and freshly ground black pepper to taste
2 tbsp Beef Bouillon (p. 2) (30 mL)
1 small bunch chives, chopped
freshly grated nutmeg to taste
2 tbsp vegetable oil (30 mL)
28 stalks asparagus, trimmed and peeled
4 Kassler (cooked smoked pork rib chops, available at
    German delicatessens)

1. Light barbecue (optional: chops may also be pan-fried).
2. Boil potatoes in salted water until tender-firm, 10 to 15 minutes. Drain and cool in a colander.
3. Following the method on p. 8, make a mayonnaise of egg yolks, mustard, vinegar, oil, salt, and pepper. Add bouillon and chives.
4. When potatoes are cool enough to handle, peel and slice them in ¼" (6-mm) rounds. Add to mayonnaise and taste for salt, pepper, and nutmeg.
5. Bring a large pot of water to a boil for asparagus.
6. Brush chops lightly with oil (they are already salted). Grill or pan-fry 5 minutes on each side.
7. Shortly before chops will be done, add asparagus to boiling water. Cover and cook 2 minutes (less if stalks are very thin). Asparagus and chops should be finished at the same time.
8. Drain well.

Presentation:
Arrange a portion of asparagus in the center of each plate, with a chop on one side and potato salad on the other.

Pork chops with mushrooms and apple purée

6 portions

6 Spartan apples
juice of 1 lemon
6 5-oz (150-g) pork loin chops, ¾ " to 1" (2 to 2.5 cm) thick
2 tbsp vegetable oil (30 mL)
salt and freshly ground pepper to taste
6 leaves fresh sage *or* ½ tsp dried (2 mL)
¼ cup butter (50 g)
2 lb fresh mushrooms, sliced (1 kg)
⅔ cup chopped parsley (30 g)
a few drops Calvados
2 tbsp butter (30 g)

1. Light barbecue (optional: chops may also be pan-fried).
2. Wash apples and slice—skins, seeds, and all—into a saucepan.
3. Pour lemon juice over apples, cover pan, and simmer until tender (about 10 minutes).
4. Purée apples and pass through a sieve, discarding skins and seeds. Return purée to saucepan and set aside.
5. Brush chops with vegetable oil and season with salt, pepper, and sage.
6. Barbecue 5 minutes on each side or pan-fry 8 minutes on each side. Test for doneness.
7. While chops cook, melt the ¼ cup (50 g) butter in a large frying pan. Add mushrooms and sauté slowly.
8. Add parsley and taste for salt and pepper. Keep warm.
9. Just before serving, warm apple purée and stir in butter and Calvados.

Presentation:
Place a portion of apple purée on each plate. Set one chop on each portion and top with sautéed mushrooms. Serve immediately.

Navarin of lamb with herb butter

6 portions

Lamb and vegetables:
2 tbsp virgin olive oil (30 mL)
2 lb lamb leg meat, cut in 1" (2.5-cm) cubes (1 kg)
mirepoix of 3 cloves garlic, 1 carrot, 1 stalk celery, 1 leek
1 large onion, finely chopped
½ small tin tomato paste
1 cup red wine (250 mL)
2 whole cloves
1 bay leaf
1 lb green peas in the pod (500 g)
2 medium potatoes

Herb butter:
1 lb room-temperature butter (450 g)
½ bunch parsley, chopped
1 sprig rosemary, chopped
1 sprig thyme, chopped
salt to taste
12 black peppercorns, crushed
juice of ½ lemon

1. In a large stewing pot or Dutch oven, heat oil to just below smoking point.
2. Spread lamb pieces in bottom of pot and sear, without stirring, 5 minutes.
3. Stir around, then sear undisturbed another 5 minutes. Transfer meat to a plate, leaving oil in pot.
4. Add mirepoix and onion and brown 10 minutes.
5. Add tomato paste and continue roasting until mixture is an even brown color.
6. Deglaze with wine and return lamb to pot. Reduce heat to a simmer and add cloves and bay leaf.
7. Add just enough water to cover. Cover pot and stew 45 minutes.

8. Meanwhile, shell and blanch peas. Turn and boil potatoes.
9. Cut butter in cubes and beat with an electric mixer until light.
10. Add herbs, salt, pepper, and lemon juice and beat 1 minute longer. Refrigerate.
11. After 45 minutes' stewing, remove meat from pot and strain sauce over it. Discard vegetables.
12. Return stew to pot and bring back to a boil. Whisk in one-quarter of the chilled herb butter. (Freeze the rest to use with grilled steak, hamburger, chicken, or fish.)

Presentation:
Place stew on a large serving platter and arrange potatoes and peas around it. Serve immediately.

Loin of lamb with leeks

4 portions

1 bunch leeks
¼ cup butter (50 g)
salt, pepper, and freshly grated nutmeg to taste
1 sprig fresh thyme, roughly chopped
¼ cup whipping (35%) cream (50 mL)
1 saddle fresh lamb, boned into loins and tenderloins (use
    bones for Lamb Jus)
1 tbsp olive oil (15 mL)
1 clove garlic, pressed
1 cup Lamb Jus (p. 4) (250 mL)
2 tbsp cold butter, cubed (25 g)

1. Light barbecue or preheat oven to 400°F (200°C).
2. Trim leeks and split lengthwise. Wash well.
3. Blanch in salted boiling water, about 1 minute. Refresh in
   cold water and chop roughly.
4. Heat butter in a saucepan. Add leeks and sauté gently 5
   minutes. Season with salt, pepper, nutmeg, and half the
   thyme.
5. Process to a medium consistency in blender or food processor
   by running machine in short bursts for about 5 seconds,
   adding cream as you go (or chop by hand).
6. Brush lamb with olive oil and season with salt, pepper, and
   garlic.
7. Grill or roast 5 minutes on each side. Remove from heat and
   let rest.
8. Boil up lamb jus. Whisk in cold butter and remaining thyme.

Presentation:
Slice lamb on the bias against the grain. Cover the center of
each plate with leek mixture and arrange slices on top. Drizzle
lamb jus around the edges and serve immediately.

MAIN COURSES: POULTRY

Roast chicken

Chicken brochettes

Coq au vin

Chicken breasts with parsley beurre blanc

Guinea fowl with lemon and almonds

Duck with olives

Roast chicken

4 portions

4-lb (2-kg) chicken (preferably yellow)
1 lemon
salt and freshly ground pepper to taste
2 tbsp olive oil (30 mL)
¼ cup dry vermouth (60 mL)
2 tbsp cold butter, cubed (30 g)
1 small sprig parsley, chopped

1. Preheat oven to 400°F (200°C).
2. Wash chicken inside and out and dry well.
3. Cut lemon in half and squeeze over chicken. Put squeezed halves in cavity.
4. Season exterior of chicken with salt and pepper.
5. Truss for roasting.
6. Add oil to roasting pan and place chicken in it, lying on one side.
7. Roast 10 minutes, then turn chicken to other side.
8. After another 10 minutes, turn chicken to lie on its back. Reduce heat and continue roasting approximately 1½ hours longer, basting from time to time.
9. Test for doneness by inserting a fork in thigh: chicken is ready when juices run clear. If no juices appear, or if they are reddish in color, continue roasting.
10. When done, cover chicken with foil and let rest 15 minutes before carving.
11. Pour off all fat from roasting pan and deglaze with vermouth.
12. Reduce liquid by one-third. Whisk in butter and parsley and keep warm.

Presentation:
Carve chicken or cut in serving pieces and serve on top of Spätzle (p. 105), with warm pan sauce on the side.

Chicken brochettes

4 portions

2 cups yogurt (500 mL)
3 cloves garlic, crushed
2 tbsp chopped fresh ginger (30 mL)
salt and freshly ground pepper to taste
juice of 2 limes
1 tbsp ground cumin (15 mL)
1 tbsp ground coriander (15 mL)
3- to 4-lb (1.5 to 2-kg) chicken
1 large Bermuda onion

1. Combine all ingredients except chicken and onion.
2. Bone chicken and cut in 1½" (4-cm) cubes.
3. Place chicken pieces in marinade and refrigerate overnight.
4. Light barbecue or preheat broiler.
5. Cut onion in wedges and place on skewers, alternating with chicken pieces.
6. Grill about 5 minutes on each side.

Presentation:
Remove from skewers and serve with rice and Salade Marocaine (p. 34).

Special equipment:
Skewers

Coq au vin

4 portions

Marinade:
6 juniper berries, crushed
12 black peppercorns, crushed
1 bottle red wine (750 mL)
1 medium onion, finely chopped
2 carrots, sliced
½ celery heart, sliced
2 bay leaves
1 small bunch fresh thyme, leaves only
1 small bunch parsley, stalks only

Chicken and vegetables:
4-lb (2-kg) chicken
½ cup butter (125 g)
2 cups Chicken Stock (p. 3) (500 mL)
7 oz pearl onions (200 g)
1 leek, well washed
1 lb mushrooms (500 g)
7 oz side bacon (200 g)

1. Three days before you plan to serve, combine all marinade ingredients in a large stainless steel bowl.
2. Separate chicken into leg and breast pieces. Cut each piece in two.
3. Add chicken pieces to marinade. Cover with waxed paper and refrigerate, turning once a day.
4. On the third day remove chicken pieces. Strain marinade and reserve both liquid and vegetables.
5. Melt butter in a large, heavy casserole and sauté chicken pieces until golden on all sides. Remove from casserole and set aside.
6. Add marinade vegetables and sauté just until brown (the sugar from the wine makes them burn easily).

7. Add marinade liquid, stock, and chicken pieces and bring to a boil.
8. Reduce heat, cover, and simmer 20 to 30 minutes, until thigh juices run clear. Remove chicken to serving dish and keep warm.
9. Increase heat to high and reduce sauce by half, skimming surface periodically to remove scum and excess grease.
10. Meanwhile, peel pearl onions and cut leek in $\frac{1}{4}''$ (12-mm) squares.
11. Quarter mushrooms and cut bacon in batons.
12. Start cooking bacon in a dry pan until it renders some fat, then add onions and mushrooms and sauté gently. (If necessary, add a little butter.)
13. Strain reduced sauce and discard marinade vegetables.
14. Add mushroom mixture to sauce and bring to a boil. Taste for salt and pepper.

Presentation:
Pour sauce over chicken and serve immediately, with boiled potatoes.

Chicken breasts with parsley beurre blanc

2 portions

¼ cup dry white wine (60 mL)
¼ cup white wine vinegar (60 mL)
5 or 6 peppercorns, crushed
1 shallot, chopped
1 bay leaf
½ cup water (125 mL)
2 tbsp roughly chopped fresh ginger (15 g)
2 boneless chicken breasts
salt to taste
¼ cup cold butter, cubed (60 g)
½ bunch Italian parsley, finely chopped

1. Place wine, vinegar, pepper, shallot, and bay leaf in a small saucepan and set aside.
2. Place water in another saucepan (similar in diameter to bamboo steamer) and add ginger.
3. Season chicken with salt to taste.
4. Place in steamer and set over water. Cover and put on high heat.
5. At the same time, put wine mixture on to boil.
6. Steam chicken until flesh loses its translucency, about 10 minutes.
7. Meanwhile, boil wine mixture until reduced to a syrup just covering bottom of pan.
8. Whisk in cold butter and add parsley.

Presentation:
Slice chicken and arrange attractively on warm plates. Nap with sauce and serve immediately.

Special equipment:
Bamboo steamer

Guinea fowl with lemon and almonds

4 portions

4 oz whole blanched almonds (125 g)
3-lb (1.5-kg) fresh guinea fowl
1 medium onion, sliced
4 tsp butter (20 g)
salt and freshly ground pepper to taste
2 cloves garlic, minced
1 lemon
¼ cup water (50 mL)

1. Preheat oven to 400°F (200°C).
2. Place almonds on a baking sheet and roast until lightly browned, about 5 minutes. Remove from oven and cool.
3. Truss fowl as for roasting chicken.
4. Gently sauté onion in butter in a large soup pot about 5 minutes.
5. Season trussed fowl with salt, pepper, and garlic. Place in soup pot, breast side down.
6. Cut lemon in slices ¼" (6 mm) thick. Place half the slices in cavity and the rest around fowl.
7. Sprinkle with toasted almonds. Pour water into bottom of pan.
8. Bring to a boil, cover, and reduce heat to a simmer. Steam approximately 2 hours, or until thigh juices run clear.

Presentation:
Place fowl on a large serving platter and remove legs. Separate drumsticks and thighs. Skin breast and carve. Remove lemon slices from pot, bring juices to a boil, and taste for salt. Pour over meat and serve immediately.

Duck with olives

4 portions

1 duck (preferably fresh)
salt and freshly ground pepper to taste
2 tbsp olive oil (30 mL)
10 oz small whole green olives (300 g)
mirepoix of 2 medium onions, 1 carrot, 2 stalks celery
2 cloves garlic, chopped
1 cup red wine (250 mL)
2 whole cloves
1 sprig fresh oregano, chopped *or* ½ tsp dried (2 mL)
2 cups Chicken Stock (p. 3) (500 mL)
2 tbsp cold butter, cubed (30 g)

1. Preheat oven to 400°F (200°C).
2. Truss duck as for roasting chicken and season with salt and pepper.
3. Place in roasting pan with olive oil and sear in oven 10 minutes on each side.
4. Turn duck on its back, reduce heat to 325°F (160°C), and roast approximately 1 hour, basting from time to time.
5. Meanwhile, pit olives and cut in rounds about ⅛" (3 mm) thick.
6. Halfway through cooking time, add mirepoix and garlic to roasting pan.
7. When duck is done, remove from pan and place on a platter to rest.
8. Continue roasting mirepoix in oven until well browned, 20 to 30 minutes.
9. Leaving mirepoix in pan, pour off all grease.

10. Deglaze with wine, add cloves and oregano, and boil to reduce by half.
11. Add chicken stock and reduce again by half.
12. Carve duck onto a warm serving platter.
13. Strain sauce and whisk in cold butter.
14. Stir in olive slices and pour over duck. Serve immediately.

MAIN COURSES: FISH AND SHELLFISH

Dover sole with brown butter and tarragon

Grouper with curried spinach

Salmon with fennel and tomatoes

Trout au bleu with boiled potatoes

Striped bass with potatoes and basil beurre blanc

Squid with lemon, parsley, and anchovies

Petite marmite de fruits de mer

Petit ragout of lobster

Dover sole with brown butter and tarragon

2 portions

¼ cup olive oil (60 mL)
2 12-oz (350-g) Dover sole, filleted
salt and freshly ground pepper to taste
flour for dredging
¼ cup butter (60 g)
juice of 1 lemon
1 sprig fresh tarragon, chopped *or* ½ tsp dried (2 mL)

1. Place oil in a large skillet and heat to just below smoking point.
2. Season fillets with salt and pepper. Sprinkle flour on a baking sheet and pass fillets through it.
3. Fry fillets in oil until golden, approximately 2 minutes on each side.
4. Remove from pan and place on two warm plates. Discard oil.
5. Return pan to heat and add butter.
6. When butter is just beginning to brown, add lemon juice and tarragon.

Presentation:
Nap butter over fillets and serve immediately, with boiled potatoes.

Grouper with curried spinach

4 portions

Fish:
14-oz (400-g) piece grouper, skinned by fishmonger
3 tbsp butter (40 g)
salt and freshly ground pepper to taste

Spinach:
1 large bunch fresh spinach
2 tbsp olive oil (30 mL)
1 tsp ground cumin (2 g)
¾ tsp ground coriander (2 g)
pinch cayenne pepper
1 clove garlic, chopped
4 tsp very finely chopped fresh ginger (10 g)
1 cup whipping (35%) cream (250 mL)
salt to taste

1. Cut grouper across the grain in 8 equal slices.
2. Pound slightly to make uniform thickness.
3. Cover a baking sheet with foil and butter it.
4. Arrange grouper slices on foil. Dot with butter, season with salt and pepper, and set aside.
5. Stem and wash spinach, changing water at least three times.
6. Blanch spinach.
7. Refresh in cold water. Squeeze dry and chop coarsely.
8. Heat oil in a skillet to just below smoking point. Add cumin, coriander, and cayenne and "roast," stirring constantly, until they just begin to change color, 1½ to 2 minutes. Stop roasting process by removing pan from heat and adding garlic and ginger.
9. Add chopped spinach and cream. Simmer and taste for salt.

10. Turn on broiler, place shelf as high as possible, and broil grouper on one side only. (The heat radiating from the pan will cook the bottom side.)
11. Remove from broiler when just cooked, after 3 to 5 minutes. Test by pulling at fish with a fork—flesh should be on the point of turning from translucent to opaque.
12. Add juices from baking pan to simmering spinach.

Presentation:
Arrange a portion of spinach in the center of each plate. Drape two slices of grouper on top and serve.

Salmon with fennel and tomatoes

4 portions

4 sheets foil, approximately 7″ × 9″ (18 × 22 cm)
julienne of 1 small bulb fennel; 2 tomatoes, blanched, peeled,
    and seeded; 1 leek; 1 carrot
4 6-oz (180-g) fillets fresh salmon
1 clove garlic, pressed
salt and freshly ground pepper to taste
1 sprig fresh tarragon
⅜ cup butter (90 g)
2 tbsp Pernod (30 mL)

1. Preheat oven to 450°F (220°C).
2. Place foil pieces shiny side down on a flat surface.
3. Reserve half the julienne mixture and place one-quarter of
   the rest in the center of each piece of foil.
4. Rub salmon fillets with pressed garlic and place one on top of
   each portion. Season with salt and pepper.
5. Cover with remaining julienne. Place a leaf of tarragon on
   top of each portion, dot with butter, and sprinkle with Pernod.
6. Fold up foil to make packages and place on a baking tray,
   spacing equally to ensure even cooking. Bake approximately
   15 minutes.

Presentation:

Slide salmon out of packages onto plates and cover with julienne and baking juices. Serve immediately.

Trout au bleu with boiled potatoes

2 portions

Court bouillon:
water
1 carrot, 1 leek, 1 stalk celery, all sliced on the bias ⅛"
    (3 mm) thick
1 medium onion, halved lengthwise and sliced ⅛"
    (3 mm) thick
2 whole cloves
1 bay leaf
12 black peppercorns, crushed
¼ cup white wine vinegar (60 mL)
salt to taste

Trout and potatoes:
4 medium potatoes
1 lemon
½ cup butter (125 mL)
2 extremely fresh rainbow trout, cleaned

1. Add enough water to a large pot or fish poacher to fill it
   halfway. Add remaining court bouillon ingredients and boil
   about 20 minutes.
2. Meanwhile, turn and boil potatoes. Cut lemon in wedges and
   melt butter.
3. Place trout in boiling court bouillon, reduce heat to a simmer,
   and poach approximately 8 minutes (if killed immediately
   before poaching, they will turn blue when cooked).

Presentation:
Serve trout whole, garnished with some of the court bouillon
ingredients and accompanied by melted butter, boiled potatoes, and lemon wedges.

Striped bass with potatoes and basil beurre blanc

2 portions

2 large potatoes, skins on
2 tbsp olive oil (25 mL)
2-lb (1-kg) striped bass, trimmed and filleted
salt and freshly ground pepper to taste
½ cup white wine vinegar (125 mL)
½ cup dry white wine (125 mL)
1 shallot, finely chopped
¼ cup cold butter, cubed (50 g)
6 leaves fresh basil, chopped

1. Light barbecue.
2. Boil potatoes in salted water until nearly tender, about 15 minutes. Drain and cool in a colander.
3. When cool, peel and cut in ½" (12-mm) slabs. Dip in olive oil and set aside.
4. Season fish with salt and pepper and brush with olive oil.
5. Place vinegar, wine, and shallot in a saucepan and bring to a boil. Reduce by half and set aside.
6. Season potato slabs with salt and pepper and place on grill to brown. Turn and brown other side.
7. Place fish fillets on grill and cook approximately 3 minutes on each side.
8. Warm sauce and whisk in cold butter and chopped basil.

Presentation:
Place grilled potatoes on plates with fillets on top. Pour wine mixture over fish and serve immediately.

Squid with lemon, parsley, and anchovies

4 portions

6 small fresh squid, cleaned by fishmonger
salt and freshly ground pepper to taste
1 tomato
1 lemon
½ cup olive oil (125 mL)
2 tbsp butter (25 g)
1 clove garlic, minced
2 anchovy fillets, minced
1 small bunch fresh parsley, finely chopped
flour for dredging

1. Cut squid in rings approximately ⅛" (3 mm) thick. Season with salt and pepper.
2. Blanch, peel, and seed tomato. Cut in ½" (12-mm) squares.
3. Fillet lemon and cut in small pieces.
4. Pour oil into a small frying pan to a depth of ⅛" (3 mm).
5. In another pan heat butter until it begins to brown. Add garlic, tomato, lemon pieces, anchovies, and parsley.
6. Heat thoroughly and transfer mixture to four warm plates.
7. Heat oil until nearly smoking.
8. Dredge squid rings in flour and, working quickly, drop into hot oil. Turn once.
9. When lightly browned on both sides (about 4 minutes), remove to paper towels to drain briefly.

Presentation:
Arrange drained squid rings on top of parsley mixture and serve immediately.

Petite marmite de fruits de mer

4 portions

Fumet:
4 tsp butter (20 g)
4 tsp olive oil (20 g)
1 clove garlic, chopped
2 cups Fish Fumet (p. 5) (500 mL)
½ phial saffron infused in 4 tsp white wine (20 mL)
salt and freshly ground pepper to taste
4 tsp Pernod (20 mL)

Garnish:
8 tiny littleneck clams, rinsed
8 medium mussels, cleaned and bearded
1 green onion, cut on the bias in very fine strips
1 clove garlic, mashed
julienne of 1 sweet red pepper, roasted and peeled (p. 113);
    ½ small bulb fennel *or* 1 stalk celery; ½ leek (white
    only); 1 tomato, blanched, peeled, and seeded
8 medium sea scallops
14 oz fresh halibut fillet, cut in 8 strips (400 g)

1. Melt butter and oil in a soup pot. Add garlic and sauté briefly.
2. Add fish fumet and bring to a boil.
3. Add clams, cover pot, and steam until they open, about 5 minutes.
4. Add prepared garnish vegetables and mussels. Cover and steam until mussels open, about 5 minutes.
5. Add scallops and halibut strips.
6. Let liquid return almost to the boil, then transfer solid ingredients to separate bowls—shellfish in one, halibut in another, vegetables in a third.

7. Bring liquid back to a boil and add saffron infusion.
8. Taste for salt and pepper and add Pernod.
9. Keep hot while you arrange garnish.

Presentation:

Arrange shellfish in their shells attractively in warm soup bowls. Place a portion of vegetables in the center of each and cover with two halibut strips. Ladle on hot fumet and serve immediately.

Petit ragout of lobster

4 portions

2 1½-lb (750-g) live lobsters
½ bulb fennel
2 medium tomatoes
12 stalks asparagus
½ lb fresh peas in the pod (250 g)
1 sprig fresh tarragon
1 tbsp olive oil (15 mL)
1 clove garlic, minced
2 shallots, finely chopped
2 tbsp white wine (30 mL)
1 cup whipping (35%) cream (250 mL)
2 tbsp cognac (30 mL)
¼ cup Lobster Butter (p. 6) (50 g)
salt and freshly ground black pepper to taste

1. Bring water to boil in a large soup pot and add a handful of salt.
2. Add live lobsters and boil, covered, 10 minutes.
3. Remove lobsters and place in sink to drain and cool. Discard cooking water.
4. When cool, remove claws and split bodies lengthwise.
5. Remove meat from tails and claws and reserve. (Use carcasses for Lobster Butter.)
6. Cut fennel in julienne.
7. Blanch tomatoes. Peel, seed, and cut in julienne.
8. Cut asparagus in 3″ (7.5-cm) tips.
9. Shell peas and pluck tarragon leaves from stem.
10. Heat oil in a saucepan and add garlic and shallots.
11. Add fennel and sauté gently 2 minutes.
12. Add wine, increase heat, and reduce to a syrupy consistency, about 2 minutes.

13. Add cream and reduce again until almost sauce consistency.
14. Add peas, asparagus, tarragon, and tomatoes.
15. Add lobster meat.
16. Add cognac and whisk in lobster butter. Taste for salt and pepper.

Presentation:

Border hot plates with Saffron Rice (p. 107). Spoon a serving of ragout into the center of each ring, making sure everybody gets one whole piece of claw meat and a portion of tail. Serve very hot.

SIDE DISHES

Fettuccine with chives

Fusilli with Crotonese and herbs

Spätzle

Mushroom risotto

Saffron rice

Asparagus with mustard and tarragon

Fresh green peas braised with mint and chiffonade of lettuce

Green beans with parsley cream

Braised leeks with marrow

Potato and turnip gratiné with chèvre

Roasted peppers with garlic and oregano

Sautéed eggplant vinaigrette

Vegetable brochettes

Fettuccine with chives

2 portions

1 tbsp salt (15 mL)
1 tbsp butter (15 g)
2 tbsp sour cream *or* Crème Fraîche (p. 10) (25 mL)
1 small bunch fresh chives, finely chopped
salt, pepper, and freshly grated nutmeg to taste
7 oz fresh fettuccine (200 g) *or* 4 oz dried (125 g)

1. Add salt to a large pot of water and bring to a rolling boil.
2. Meanwhile, place butter, cream, chives, and seasonings in a stainless steel bowl and set over pot to heat ingredients.
3. When water is ready, add fettuccine and cook until al dente.
4. Drain fettuccine. Add to ingredients in bowl and mix well.

Presentation:
Serve immediately, either on its own or with a meat dish such as Ossobuco (p. 72) or Veal Kidney (p. 74).

Fusilli with Crotonese and herbs

6 portions

1 tomato, blanched, peeled, and seeded
1 clove garlic, minced
1 sprig parsley, chopped
1 sprig thyme, chopped
¼ cup butter (50 g)
¼ cup ricotta cheese (50 g)
freshly grated nutmeg to taste
10 oz Italian fusilli (300 g)
1 cup freshly grated Crotonese *or* Parmesan cheese (75 g)

1. Bring a large pot of salted water to a boil.
2. Place all ingredients except fusilli and cheese in a large bowl.
3. When water reaches a rolling boil, add fusilli and cook until al dente, about 8 minutes.
4. Drain fusilli and add to bowl.
5. Add cheese and mix well.

Presentation:
Place in warm soup bowls and serve immediately as an accompaniment to grilled meats or Ossobuco (p. 72).

Spätzle

4 portions

3 eggs
1 ¾ cups flour (250 g)
salt and freshly grated nutmeg to taste
up to 2 tbsp milk (30 mL)
¼ cup butter (50 g)

1. Make a paste of eggs and flour.
2. Add salt and nutmeg. Slowly add milk and work dough into a satiny, elastic mass.
3. Bring a large pot of salted water to a boil. Extrude dough into water one-third at a time and cook until spätzle rise to the surface.
4. Scoop out each batch, refresh in cold water, and place on paper towels to dry.
5. Just before serving, melt butter in non-stick frying pan and sauté spätzle about 5 minutes, stirring frequently. Season with salt and serve.

Special equipment:
Spätzle extruder
Non-stick frying pan

Mushroom risotto

2 portions

1 tbsp olive oil (15 mL)
½ cup Italian *or* arborio rice (85 g)
1 small onion, chopped
2 cloves garlic, minced
1 cup Chicken Stock (p. 3) *or* commercial bouillon
    (250 mL)
2 tbsp white wine (25 mL)
1 cup thickly sliced mushrooms (75 g)
¼ bunch parsley, chopped
pinch fresh sage
1 green onion, sliced
salt and freshly ground pepper to taste
½ cup freshly grated Parmesan cheese (35 g)

1. Heat oil in a heavy-bottomed sauté pan. Add rice and shake until grains just begin to brown (one or two may pop).
2. Remove from heat and add onion and garlic to stop searing process.
3. Return pan to heat and adjust to a simmer. Slowly add one-third of the stock and cook, stirring occasionally, until almost all liquid has been absorbed. Repeat with remaining stock (rice should still have a very slight crunch).
4. Add wine and remaining ingredients, finishing with Parmesan. The texture should be slightly liquid—not too runny, but not too dry.

Presentation:
Serve either on its own or as an accompaniment to grilled meats.

Saffron rice

6 portions

1 tbsp butter (15 g)
1 onion, finely chopped
1 ¼ cups basmati rice (250 g)
2 ½ cups Chicken Stock (p. 3) (double the volume of rice)
½ phial saffron threads
salt to taste

1. Preheat oven to 350°F (180°C).
2. Melt butter in a saucepan. Add onion and sauté gently 5 minutes.
3. Add rice and stir well.
4. Add stock, saffron, and salt. Slowly bring to a boil, stirring occasionally.
5. Cover and place in oven for ½ hour, or until all liquid has been absorbed.

Presentation:
Serve with Petit Ragout of Lobster (p. 100).

Asparagus with mustard and tarragon

4 portions

28 stalks asparagus, evenly sized
2 egg yolks
2 tbsp tarragon vinegar (30 mL)
4 peppercorns, coarsely ground
1 shallot, chopped
½ cup butter (125 g)
1 tbsp Dijon mustard (15 mL)
¼ cup whipping (35%) cream (50 mL)
salt to taste

1. Peel bottom halves of asparagus. Trim ends to make stalks an even length.
2. Place egg yolks in a stainless steel bowl.
3. Combine vinegar, pepper, and shallot in a saucepan over high heat and boil until reduced by half.
4. Strain reduction and reserve.
5. Melt butter in a saucepan and keep warm but not hot.
6. Whisk mustard and strained reduction into egg yolks.
7. Bring a large pot of salted water to boil, to use as indirect heat for cooking the sauce and to boil the asparagus.
8. Whisk yolk mixture over boiling water until thickened to the consistency of mayonnaise.
9. Whisk in warm melted butter and cream. Taste sauce for salt and keep warm.
10. Add asparagus to boiling water and cook 2 to 3 minutes, to desired crunchiness.

Presentation:
Ladle a pool of sauce onto each of four large plates. Arrange seven stalks of asparagus attractively over each portion and serve immediately.

Fresh green peas braised with mint and chiffonade of lettuce

4 portions

1 lb fresh peas in the pod (500 g)
1 small head leaf lettuce
1 small bunch fresh mint
⅓ cup butter (75 g)
2 shallots, finely chopped
salt and freshly ground pepper to taste

1. Shell peas.
2. Cut lettuce in chiffonade.
3. Chop mint roughly.
4. Melt butter in a saucepan and gently sauté shallots 3 minutes.
5. Add, in this order, lettuce, peas, and mint.
6. Cover and braise gently, on low heat, 6 minutes.
7. Taste for salt and pepper.

Presentation:
Serve in a warm vegetable dish, as an accompaniment to roasted or grilled meat or fish.

Green beans with parsley cream

6 portions

1 ¼ lb fresh green beans (550 g)
2 ⅔ cups fresh parsley (120 g)
¼ cup butter (60 g)
⅔ cup whipping (35%) cream (150 mL)
salt and freshly ground pepper to taste

1. Blanch beans in salted water, about 3 minutes. Refresh and hull ends.
2. Blanch parsley and refresh in cold water.
3. Drain parsley, squeeze dry, and chop finely.
4. Put butter, chopped parsley, beans, and cream in a small saucepan.
5. Cover and simmer until heated through, about 5 minutes.
6. Taste for salt and pepper.

Presentation:
Serve as an accompaniment to veal dishes or roast lamb, or alone as a vegetable course.

Braised leeks with marrow

4 portions

4 small leeks
2 tbsp butter (25 g)
1 tbsp white wine vinegar (15 mL)
½ cup Beef Bouillon (p. 2) (125 mL)
1 small sprig thyme, chopped
salt and freshly ground pepper to taste
approximately 1 lb marrow bones (500 g)
⅓ cup freshly grated Parmesan cheese (25 g)
⅔ cup fine white bread crumbs (30 g)

1. Slit leeks in half lengthwise. Taking care to keep halves intact, wash under running water, scrubbing gently and making sure every layer is rinsed.
2. Blanch in salted boiling water, 1 minute. Refresh and drain.
3. Grease baking dish lightly with 1 tsp (5 mL) of the butter.
4. Cut leeks in 2″ (5-cm) lengths and place in dish.
5. Preheat oven to 350°F (180°C).
6. Mix vinegar with bouillon. Add thyme, salt, and pepper, and pour over leeks.
7. Use your thumb to push marrow out of bones (discard bones).
8. Chop marrow and remaining butter and sprinkle over leeks.
9. Bake ½ hour. Remove from oven and turn on broiler.
10. Sprinkle leeks with cheese and crumbs and place under broiler until top is golden, about 5 minutes.

Presentation:
Serve immediately with roasted or grilled meat.

Special equipment:
8″ (20-cm) square oven-proof baking dish

Potato and turnip gratiné with chèvre

4 portions

¾ lb potatoes (350 g)
¾ lb white turnips (350 g)
1 small onion
4 oz French chèvre (125 g)
4 tsp butter (20 g)
salt and freshly ground pepper to taste
½ tsp freshly grated nutmeg (2 mL)
¾ cup whipping (35%) cream (175 mL)

1. Peel potatoes and turnips and slice about ⅛" (3 mm) thick.
2. Chop onion finely.
3. Crumble chèvre.
4. Preheat oven to 350°F (180°C).
5. Grease gratin dish with butter.
6. Sprinkle with some chopped onion.
7. Cover with a layer of potato slices. Follow with a layer of turnip slices.
8. Season with salt, pepper, and nutmeg.
9. Pour in some cream.
10. Sprinkle with some crumbled chèvre.
11. Repeat steps 6, 7, 8, 9, and 10 until dish is full nearly to the brim.
12. Slowly pour in any remaining cream.
13. Top with remaining chèvre and onions.
14. Bake 30 to 40 minutes, until bubbly and golden.

Presentation:
Remove from oven and place directly on a heat-proof mat on the table.

Special equipment:
Round ceramic gratin dish approximately 6" (15 cm) in diameter and 2" (5 cm) deep

Roasted peppers with garlic and oregano

6 portions

2 cloves garlic, minced
1 small bunch fresh oregano, chopped (about 1 tbsp/15 mL)
    or ½ tsp dried (2 mL)
1 ¼ cups olive oil (300 mL)
salt to taste
4 sweet red peppers
4 yellow banana peppers
4 pale yellow Hungarian peppers

1. Light barbecue or preheat broiler.
2. Place garlic and oregano in a large bowl. Add oil and salt and mix well.
3. When coals are white (or broiler is very hot) grill all three kinds of peppers, turning periodically, until well charred, 15 to 20 minutes.
4. Remove from heat and cover with a clean dish towel to cool and facilitate peeling.
5. Peel off skins but leave peppers intact.
6. Add to oil mixture and toss gently. (Can be prepared ahead of time and served at room temperature.)

Presentation:
Place marinated peppers on a platter in the middle of the table and let guests help themselves. Serve with beer and plenty of good bread. (Great for picnics.)

Sautéed eggplant vinaigrette

4 portions

1 eggplant
salt
1 sweet red pepper
1 clove garlic
1 small shallot
1 sprig Italian parsley
1 sprig oregano
½ cup virgin olive oil (125 mL)
2 tbsp red wine vinegar (30 mL)
2 tbsp lemon juice (30 mL)
flour for dredging
3 tbsp olive oil for sautéing (45 mL)
freshly ground pepper to taste

1. Peel eggplant and slice about ½" (12 mm) thick.
2. Sprinkle slices liberally with salt and let sit in a bowl for 30 minutes.
3. Roast red pepper under broiler, turning occasionally, until black on all sides, about 15 minutes.
4. Remove from broiler, cover with a clean cloth, and let sit until cool (the steam that collects helps loosen the skin).
5. Peel and seed pepper.
6. Slice into strips ¼" (6 mm) wide and 2" (5 cm) long and place in a bowl.
7. Chop garlic, shallot, parsley, and oregano and add to bowl.
8. Add oil, vinegar, and lemon juice and mix well.
9. Rinse eggplant slices thoroughly and pat dry on paper towels. (Taste a corner of one slice for excessive salt—you may need to rinse again.)
10. Dredge slices in flour and sauté in olive oil until golden on each side. Lay on a rack to cool just enough to handle.
11. Add slices to marinade and toss. Taste for pepper.

Presentation:
Serve either warm or at room temperature.

Vegetable brochettes

4 portions

1 small eggplant
1 medium zucchini
8 medium mushrooms
8 cherry tomatoes
⅓ cup olive oil (80 mL)
juice of 1 lemon
1 clove garlic, chopped
2 sprigs summer savory, chopped *or* ¼ tsp dried (1 mL)
salt and freshly ground pepper to taste.

1. Peel eggplant. Wash other vegetables.
2. Cut eggplant and zucchini in 1″ (2.5 cm) square pieces and sprinkle liberally with salt.
3. Combine oil, lemon juice, garlic, and savory in an oblong cake pan.
4. Rinse eggplant and zucchini thoroughly.
5. Arrange vegetables on skewers and place in pan to marinate for 1 hour.
6. Light barbecue.
7. Season vegetables with salt and pepper.
8. Grill, turning frequently, until slightly charred on all sides.
9. Serve immediately, on skewers.

Special equipment:
Wooden skewers

DESSERTS

Crème fraîche quenelles with raspberry purée
and chocolate sauce

Bittersweet chocolate mousse with clementine glaze

Vanilla mousse

Raspberry crème fraîche tart

Apple crêpes with chestnut ice cream

Profiteroles with chocolate and orange

Fruit gratiné with Grand Marnier sabayon and chocolate sauce

Marzipan and apple pastry with warmed sour cherries

Warmed sour cherries

Waffles with fresh fruit and crème fraîche

Chestnut ice cream

Coconut and passionfruit sorbet

Pear sorbet

Vin nouveau sorbet

Frozen chocolate génoise praliné with rhumtopf

Rhumtopf

Pears poached in red wine

Poached pears with caramel sauce

Chocolate walnut cake

Crème fraîche quenelles with raspberry purée and chocolate sauce

4 portions

¼ recipe Sweet Crème Fraîche (p. 10)
7 oz raspberries, fresh *or* frozen without sugar (200 g)
2 tbsp sugar (30 g)
7 oz bittersweet chocolate (200 g)
⅔ cup homogenized milk (150 mL)

1. Two days before you plan to serve, prepare crème fraîche.
2. If using fresh berries, set aside half of them for garnishing and process the rest in a blender or food processor, adding sugar as you go. (If using frozen berries, process all of them.)
3. Place chocolate and milk in a stainless steel bowl over simmering water until melted, stirring occasionally.
4. The crème fraîche will now be set to roughly the consistency of ice cream. To make quenelles, dip a teaspoon in hot water, hold it on a slant, concave side down, and draw it over the surface so that the crème follows its curve, forming an oval mound. Place directly on prepared dessert plate. Remember to redip spoon for each quenelle.

Presentation:
Pour enough berry purée onto each dessert plate to cover the bottom. Sprinkle whole berries on top. Arrange three quenelles around each portion of berries. Finally, drizzle chocolate sauce over half of each quenelle.

Bittersweet chocolate mousse with clementine glaze

6 portions

Mousse:
7 oz bittersweet Swiss chocolate (200 g)
7 oz unsweetened baking chocolate (200 g)
¼ cup milk (50 mL)
5 eggs, separated
⅔ cup sugar, divided (150 g)
1 tsp salt (5 mL)
¼ cup amber rum (60 mL)
2 cups whipping (35%) cream (500 mL)

Glaze:
12 clementines (you can substitute grapefruit, tangerines, or oranges)
⅓ cup cold unsalted butter (75 g)

1. Break both kinds of chocolate into a stainless steel bowl and add milk. Set over simmering water to melt.
2. Place egg yolks in another stainless steel bowl and add half the sugar. Whisk over a simmering bain-marie until light in color and the consistency of mayonnaise.
3. Whisk melted chocolate into yolk mixture. Add salt and rum and set aside.
4. Whip egg whites until stiff, adding remaining sugar halfway through.
5. Whip cream until stiff.
6. Fold beaten whites into chocolate mixture.
7. Fold in whipped cream. Cover and refrigerate about 4 hours, until set.

8. Meanwhile, juice clementines.
9. Place juice in a saucepan and boil until reduced by three-quarters. Whisk in cold butter until melted. Remove from heat.

Presentation:
Form mousse into quenelles (p. 117) and place one or two on each plate. Surround with warm clementine glaze and serve.

Vanilla mousse

6 portions

4 leaves *or* 1 package gelatin
1 tbsp cold water (15 mL)
8 egg yolks
⅔ cup sugar (150 g)
1 vanilla bean, split lengthwise and scooped out
2 tbsp Galliano (30 mL)
2 tsp pure vanilla extract (10 mL)
2 cups whipping (35%) cream (500 mL)

1. Soak gelatin in cold water.
2. Place egg yolks in a stainless steel bowl and add sugar.
3. Whisk over a simmering bain-marie until light in color and the consistency of mayonnaise.
4. Add soaked gelatin, vanilla scrapings, Galliano, and vanilla extract. Mix well and set aside.
5. Whip cream until stiff and fold into yolk mixture.
6. Cover with plastic wrap and refrigerate 4 hours, or until set.

Presentation:
Form mousse into quenelles (p. 117) and serve two or three on each plate, surrounded with fresh berries, Warmed Sour Cherries (p. 120), or Rhumtopf (p. 135). You might also set a Meringue (p. 11) on each side of the quenelles.

Raspberry crème fraîche tart

8 portions

14 oz Sweet Pastry (p. 16) (400 g)
2 ½ pints fresh raspberries (1250 mL)
1 cup Sweet Crème Fraîche (p. 10) (250 mL)
optional: 2 tbsp framboise eau de vie *or* kirsch (30 mL)
6 oz apricot jam (180 g)

1. Preheat oven to 375°F (190°C).
2. Roll pastry to a thickness of approximately ⅛″ (3 mm).
3. Roll onto rolling pin and unroll over tart pan. Push pastry into corners and up sides, then roll pin over top of pan to trim off excess pastry (freeze it for later use).
4. Place a sheet of parchment paper in pastry form and cover with dried beans. Bake approximately ½ hour, or until edges are golden brown. Remove from oven and cool thoroughly at room temperature. Remove beans and paper (save for another time).
5. Purée 1 cup (250 mL) of the raspberries and reserve the rest.
6. Combine purée with crème fraîche and optional eau de vie. Spread into cooled pastry shell.
7. Arrange reserved berries over surface and chill 2 hours.
8. Place jam in a small saucepan and melt over low heat. Drizzle over berries.

Presentation:
Remove rim from pan and place tart on a cake platter. Cut in wedges and serve either plain or with a dollop of unsweetened whipped cream.

Special equipment:
Tart pan with removable rim

Apple crêpes with chestnut ice cream

4 portions

½ recipe Chestnut Ice Cream (p. 130)
1 recipe Crêpe batter (p. 12)
3 Spy apples, peeled and coarsely grated
2 tbsp sugar (30 g)
2 tbsp Calvados (30 mL)
2 tbsp butter (30 g)

1. Make ice cream and store in freezer.
2. Make crêpe batter. Add apple, sugar, and Calvados.
3. Melt butter in an 8″ (20-cm) non-stick pan and fry crêpes. Keep warm in oven.

Presentation:
Transfer crêpes to warm dessert plates and place a scoop of ice cream in the center of each. Fold in half and serve immediately.

Profiteroles with chocolate and orange

4 portions

½ recipe Choux Pastry (p. 14)
zest and juice of 2 oranges
2 tbsp sugar (30 mL)
1 cup Crème Anglaise (p. 9) (250 mL)
½ recipe Bittersweet Chocolate Mousse (p. 118)
confectioners' (icing) sugar in a sieve

1. Preheat oven to 400°F (200°C).
2. Pipe 12 small rosettes of choux pastry onto a baking tray lined with parchment paper and bake until puffy and golden, about ½ hour.
3. Combine orange zest and juice with sugar in a small saucepan and cook over low heat until sugar melts. Mix with crème anglaise and set aside.
4. When profiteroles are done, let cool 3 minutes, then slice off tops and reserve.
5. Pipe chocolate mousse into profiteroles and replace tops.

Presentation:
Spoon a pool of orange sauce onto each plate. Place three profiteroles on top, sprinkle with confectioners' sugar, and serve.

Fruit gratiné with Grand Marnier sabayon and chocolate sauce

4 portions

Fruit:
1 grapefruit
1 large navel orange
1 pint strawberries (500 mL)
1 pint raspberries (500 mL)
2 ripe Bartlett pears
2 tbsp Grand Marnier (30 mL)

Sabayon:
3 egg yolks
⅓ cup sugar (75 g)
2 tbsp Grand Marnier (30 mL)
⅔ cup whipping (35%) cream (150 mL)

Chocolate sauce:
7 oz bittersweet chocolate (200 g)
⅔ cup homogenized milk (150 mL)

1. Peel and section grapefruit and orange.
2. Hull berries.
3. Peel, core, and slice pears.
4. Place fruit in bowl, add Grand Marnier, and toss.
5. Place egg yolks and sugar in a stainless steel bowl.
6. Whisk over a simmering bain-marie until mixture is light in color and forms a ribbon when dribbled. Remove from heat, add Grand Marnier, and cool.
7. Whip cream until stiff and fold into yolk mixture.

8. Place chocolate and milk in another bowl over simmering water until melted, stirring occasionally.
9. Turn on broiler.
10. Place macerated fruit in center of dinner plates and barely cover with sabayon.
11. Place under broiler and gratiné until golden.

Presentation:
Immediately before serving, make a stream of chocolate sauce around each plate just inside the rim.

Marzipan and apple pastry with warmed sour cherries

16 portions

Pastry:
½ recipe Puff Pastry (p. 15)
1 egg, lightly beaten
4 oz whole blanched almonds (125 g)
large crystal sugar

Filling:
8 apples (preferably Spy)
⅓ cup melted butter (75 g)
½ cup (packed) brown sugar (100 g)
¼ cup Calvados (60 mL)
pinch cinnamon
pinch salt

Marzipan:
7 oz marzipan (from Denmark or Lübeck, West Germany)
    (200 g)
2 tbsp kirsch *or* maraschino liqueur (30 mL)
confectioners' (icing) sugar in a sieve

Cherries
1 recipe Warmed Sour Cherries (p. 127)

1. Preheat oven to 400°F (200°C).
2. Line a 12″ × 18″ (30- × 45-cm) baking pan with silicone or parchment paper.
3. Roll half the puff pastry into a rectangle the same size and fit into pan.
4. Dust working surface with sifted confectioners' sugar and knead marzipan. Sprinkle with liqueur and work with your hands until all liquid has been absorbed and marzipan is malleable enough to roll without breaking.

5. Roll half the marzipan into a thin rectangle the same size as pan and place on top of pastry.
6. Peel and core apples and slice into a bowl.
7. Add butter, sugar, Calvados, cinnamon, and salt. Mix well.
8. Mound apple mixture on top of marzipan, leaving approximately 1" (2.5 cm) uncovered on all sides.
9. Repeat step 5 with remaining marzipan.
10. Brush edges with beaten egg and repeat step 3.
11. Brush top of pastry with egg and decorate with almonds. Sprinkle with sugar crystals.
12. Bake 40 minutes, or until golden brown. Cool at least 1 hour before slicing.

Presentation:
Serve slices of pastry surrounded by warmed sour cherries.

Warmed Sour Cherries

6 portions

1 quart sour cherries (1 L)
½ cup sugar (100 g)
¼ cup kirsch (60 mL)

1. Wash, hull, and pit cherries.
2. Place in a saucepan with sugar and bring to a boil.
3. Cook 5 minutes, remove from heat, and add kirsch.

Presentation:
Serve with Marzipan and Apple Pastry (above), Vanilla Mousse (p. 118), or Vanilla Ice Cream (p. 9).

Waffles with fresh fruit and crème fraîche

6 portions

¼ recipe Sweet Crème Fraîche (p. 10)
10 oz fresh fruit (300 g): ½ pint strawberries (250 mL); 1
    large grapefruit; 1 large mango (you can substitute
    other fruits as long as you use at least one kind of
    berry, one citrus variety for acidity, and one pulpy
    fruit such as mango, peach, banana, even
    pineapple—just keep color and texture in mind)

Waffles:
2 egg yolks
2 cups milk (500 mL)
2 cups all-purpose flour (500 mL)
1 tbsp baking powder (15 mL)
½ tsp salt (2 mL)
⅓ cup vegetable oil (75 mL)
2 egg whites
melted butter

1. Two days before you plan to serve, prepare crème fraîche.
2. Hull berries.
3. Skin and section grapefruit.
4. Peel and slice mango.
5. Mix all fruits together.
6. Combine all ingredients for waffles except egg whites and
   melted butter.
7. Beat egg whites until stiff and fold into batter.

8. Heat waffle iron and brush both top and bottom elements lightly with melted butter.
9. Spoon in batter and cook 2 to 3 minutes, until steaming stops and waffle comes away easily from top of iron.
10. To keep cooked waffles warm, place in a single layer in a 200°F (95°C) oven; don't stack them, or they'll lose their crispness.

Presentation:
Spread some crème fraîche on each hot waffle. Spoon fruit on top and serve immediately.

Special equipment:
Waffle iron

Chestnut ice cream

6 portions

12 fresh chestnuts
⅜ cup whipping (35%) cream (90 mL)
2 tbsp honey (30 mL)
2 cups Crème Anglaise (p. 9) (500 mL)

1. Preheat oven to 400°F (200°C).
2. Score the shell of each chestnut along the grain and place on a baking sheet in oven for about 10 minutes.
3. Remove from oven. When cool enough to handle, take meat from shells.
4. Place in a small saucepan with cream and honey.
5. Bring to a boil and cook 5 minutes.
6. Purée mixture in a blender or food processor with metal blade.
7. Combine with crème anglaise and freeze in sorbétière.

Special equipment:
Sorbétière

Coconut and passionfruit sorbet

6 portions

12 ripe passionfruit
approximately 1 ½ cups water (375 mL)
1 medium coconut
1 cup sugar (250 mL)

1. Cut passionfruit in half and scoop out flesh. Reserve shells in refrigerator.
2. Push flesh through a strainer into a bowl, adding some of the water, a little at a time, to ease the straining process and make a mush. Reserve about one-quarter of the seeds (they are edible) and add to mush.
3. Crack coconut in half and reserve liquid. Remove flesh from shell.
4. Grate flesh finely. Mix with coconut liquid and water to make a mush.
5. Press coconut mush through cheesecloth and reserve the resulting milk, along with about one-tenth of the fiber.
6. Add coconut milk to passionfruit mush, then add enough water to bring the total volume to 6 cups (1500 mL).
7. Add sugar and reserved coconut fiber. (Mixture should taste slightly sweeter than you would expect; it will be less sweet after freezing.)
8. Freeze mixture in sorbétière.

Presentation:
Pipe sorbet into reserved passionfruit shells and serve immediately.

Special equipment:
Sorbétière

Pear sorbet

4 portions

4 underripe pears (preferably Bartlett)
½ cup sugar (125 mL)
¼ cup pear eau de vie (60 mL)
1 cup white wine (250 mL)
1 ripe pear for garnishing

1. Peel pears and cut roughly into saucepan.
2. Add sugar and cook slowly until tender.
3. Purée mixture and pass through a sieve.
4. Add pear eau de vie and enough white wine to bring the total volume to 6 cups (1500 mL).
5. Freeze in sorbétière.

Presentation:
To serve, pipe into champagne flutes or make quenelles (p. 117) in tulip glasses. Garnish each portion with a slice of pear.

Special equipment:
Sorbétière

Vin nouveau sorbet

8 portions as a sorbet course; 4 portions as a dessert

1 bottle vin nouveau (750 mL)
Sugar Syrup (p. 10) to taste
seedless green grapes for garnishing

1. Combine wine and sugar syrup and freeze in sorbétière. (Because of the alcohol content, this sorbet takes longer to freeze than the water-based kind.)
2. To serve, pipe into champagne flutes or make quenelles (p. 117) in tulip glasses. Garnish each portion with half a grape.

Variations:
Substitute Chardonnay, Gewürtztraminer, or Riesling.

Special equipment:
Sorbétière

Frozen chocolate génoise praliné with rhumtopf

12 portions

¾ cup freshly shelled hazelnuts (100 g)
⅞ cup sugar (200 g)
1 tbsp water (15 mL)
½ recipe Vanilla Ice Cream (Crème Anglaise, p. 9), slightly
   softened
1 recipe Chocolate Génoise (p. 13)
4 cups Rhumtopf (p. 135) (1 L)

1. Preheat oven to 375°F (190°C).
2. Place hazelnuts on a baking sheet and roast until golden, about 5 minutes (watch carefully, or they'll burn). Cool and rub off skins.
3. Combine sugar and water in a saucepan and cook over high heat until sugar turns amber. Add hazelnuts and remove from heat.
4. Transfer praliné mixture to a buttered stainless steel bowl to cool.
5. When cool, break into pieces and, using a blender or food processor, process to a powder (or wrap in a dish towel and pulverize with the broad side of a cleaver).
6. Fold praliné powder into ice cream and place in freezer.
7. Place terrine form in freezer to cool.
8. Cut 4 pieces of génoise the same size as terrine and about ½″ (12 mm) thick.
9. With a rubber spatula spread a ½″ (12-mm) layer of ice cream in bottom of chilled terrine. Cover with a layer of génoise.
10. Working quickly, repeat step 9 until terrine is full. Cover and place in freezer for at least 4 hours.

Presentation:
Cut in slices and place in the center of dessert plates. Surround with rhumtopf and serve immediately.

Special equipment:
12″ × 4″ × 3″ (35- × 10- × 7.5-cm) terrine form or meatloaf pan

Rhumtopf

approximately 1 gallon (4 L)

2 pints strawberries (1 L)
1 pint white currants (500 mL)
1 pint red currants (500 mL)
1 pint blueberries (500 mL)
2 pints raspberries (1 L)
1 pint blackberries (500 mL)
1 pint apricots (500 mL)
2 pints sour cherries (1 L)
40 oz amber rum (1200 mL)
optional: 1 green (unripe) walnut (do not substitute a
     ripe walnut)
½ part sugar to each part fruit

1. As each fruit comes into season, place the recommended amount in a large ceramic crock with half its volume of sugar.
2. Pour in enough rum to cover the fruit, cover crock, and store in refrigerator.
3. Repeat with each fruit as it becomes available.
4. Add the green walnut last—it gives the rhumtopf a special flavor.
5. Let rhumtopf sit in refrigerator until at least Christmas before using. It will keep indefinitely.

Pears poached in red wine

4 portions

1 cup red wine (250 mL)
juice of ½ lemon
¼ cup sugar (50 g)
1 vanilla bean, split lengthwise and scooped out
4 Bosc pears, stems intact

1. Combine all ingredients except pears in a stainless steel pot.
2. Peel pears with a paring knife, keeping their shape.
3. Using a parisienne knife (melon-baller), scoop out cores from the bottom, so pears look intact. Place in wine mixture.
4. Simmer gently 20 minutes, turning pears periodically so they absorb equal color on all sides. Test: the degree of ripeness will determine the cooking time.
5. Stop poaching when pears are soft but still in one piece. Cool in wine mixture.

Presentation:
Serve on a dish in a shallow pool of the poaching liquid. (This is a good accompaniment for cheeses such as Stilton, Roquefort, Gorgonzola, Cambozola, and chèvre.)

Poached pears with caramel sauce

4 portions

Pears:
1 cup white wine (250 mL)
1 vanilla bean, split lengthwise and scooped out
4 medium Bosc pears, not quite ripe, stems intact

Sauce:
⅔ cup white sugar (150 g)
¼ cup water (50 mL)
half the poaching liquid from pears
½ cup whipping (35%) cream (125 mL)

1. Place wine and vanilla bean in a saucepan.
2. Peel pears with a paring knife, keeping their shape.
3. Using a parisienne knife (melon-baller), scoop out cores from the bottom.
4. Place pears stem-up in wine, cover, and poach gently 20 minutes. Test: pears are ready when soft. The degree of ripeness will determine cooking time.
5. When done, remove pears and reserve half the poaching liquid for sauce.
6. Place sugar and water in a saucepan and boil vigorously without stirring. Watch carefully as sugar begins to change color—it burns quickly.
7. When sugar is a light amber shade, remove pan from heat and add poaching liquid all at once (it will hiss and spatter). Return to heat and add cream.
8. Simmer sauce until all lumps are gone.

Presentation:
Pour warm sauce onto dessert plates and place pears standing up in the center.

Chocolate walnut cake

8" (20-cm) cake

5 eggs
⅔ cup granulated sugar (150 g)
¾ cup cake flour, sifted (100 g)
14 oz freshly ground almonds (400 g)
3½ oz freshly ground walnuts (100 g)
10 oz semi-sweet chocolate, broken in small pieces (300 g)

1. Preheat oven to 375°F (190°C). Grease and flour an 8" (20-cm) springform pan.
2. Combine eggs and sugar and beat with a wire whip until frothy, about 5 minutes.
3. Fold in flour, almonds, and walnuts.
4. Fold in chocolate pieces.
5. Pour into pan and bake approximately 45 minutes, or until golden brown.

Presentation:
Serve warm with Vanilla Ice Cream (p. 9) and fresh fruits such as raspberries, blueberries, or peaches.

INDEX

THE JAMIE KENNEDY
COOKBOOK